R. D. Bartlett and Patricia Bartlett

Designer Reptiles and Amphibians

BARRON'S

Filled with Full-color Ph

CONTENTS

INTRODUCTION

When hobbyists first began to keep reptiles and amphibians, any suggestion that selective breeding would create an entire subset of hobbyists would have been greeted by amused hoots of disbelief. Today, almost any hobbyist either has kept a color morph or has thought seriously about it.

In our childhood, many of our most memorable tales began with some combination of the words "long, long ago, in a land far away," and ended with "and they lived happily ever after." In our tale, however, the lead-in would have to read "a short time ago, in a not-so-distant land..." and no ending could yet be written. Although it seems fanciful, this is a true story about pink snakes, blue treefrogs, and white turtles.

Our tale is about both naturally occurring color and pattern aberrancies of reptiles and amphibians and the designer colors now produced in herpetoculture, the engineered breeding of reptiles and amphibians in captivity. The tale has been unfolding in serious fashion for only about 40 years.

Early on, herpetoculturists (or herpers, as they were then called) were satisfied—

Albino examples of the western diamondback rattlesnake, Crotalus atrox, are pretty but treacherous.

delighted, in fact—to simply get snakes to breed. As a group, herpetoculturists were just beginning to overcome the barriers associated with accurately sexing snakes and other reptiles and amphibians, and to learn of the various stimuli needed to cycle the least demanding species reproductively. Since snakes were of interest to a proportionately greater number of hobbyists than other reptiles and amphibians, and had also proven the easiest of the groups to breed, it was natural that snakes were the leaders in this growing industry.

But even with all of this now said, aspiring to breed snakes was, in those early days, a lofty and admirable goal that was fraught with uncertainty. After learning the importance of natural physical parameters such as rainfall and day length in stimulating the reproductive behavior, the most successful herpetoculturists became ecologists. Efforts were made to replicate in captivity the natural conditions in which the species with which they were working were most often found in the wild. Such

parameters as seasonal temperatures, seasonal humidity, and photoperiod became the subject of research and were integral to success. Breeders looked at each other, nodded in satisfaction, and thought, "We've got it made, now."

Then came the albinos, and the hubris began all over again.

Albinos of many species of reptiles and amphibians were well known to hobbyists, but until the late 1960s and early 1970s, there was little, if any, effort to incorporate genetics and color mutations into any breeding programs.

My, how things have changed in four decades! Today (2001), although some color variants still appear spontaneously, most mutations are the result of concerted herpeto-cultural efforts. There are now more than 30 designer colors of corn snakes, a half dozen or more of black rat snakes, about a dozen variants of California kingsnake, 12 or 15 hobbyist-

As the most popular pet snake in history, entire books have been devoted to the designer colors of the corn snake, Elaphe guttata guttata. *The Gourmet Rodent produced this ruby-freckled morph.*

derived colors of leopard geckos, a few fat-tailed gecko variants, and even some albino frogs.

With the passing of each year, as our knowledge of genetics and other factors continues to increase, the drive by hobbyists to produce new and spectacular colors, patterns, intergrades, and hybrids burgeons. The result is that more and more designer morphs of more and more species make their appearance in the pet trade.

We have also learned that the gender of some reptiles—turtles and lizards specifically—is temperature-determined, rather than genetically determined. With that knowledge came

Above: This is a pretty albino-banded California kingsnake.

Right: Half black, half white, striped, banded, and many other color and pattern aberrancies in the California kingsnake are now available.

the ability to produce leopard geckos or red-eared turtles of a given sex, enhancing the availability of either males or females, as needed, to augment a breeding program.

Herpetoculture, the breeding of reptiles and amphibians in captivity, is a rather new facet of a long-established hobby. The keeping of reptiles and amphibians in captivity dates back hundreds of years. Depictions of exquisite vivariums are known from Victorian publications, and the building of these exquisite creations continues by some dedicated hobbyists even today.

Herpetoculture began in a small way—almost as an accident. Occasionally a female snake, lizard, or turtle, already gravid (the reptilian equivalent of pregnant) collected from the wild, would lay a clutch of eggs or give birth to babies. It was eventually discovered by hobbyists that these babies could be sold for a nominal amount. The possibility of financial gain leads to ever-increasing efforts to succeed, hence the birth of herpetoculture as the multi-million dollar a year industry we know today. Today there are more strangely and wonderfully colored and patterned designer reptiles and amphibians available to hobbyists than ever before—and the end is way over the horizon!

ETHICS

The responsible reptile or amphibian keeper has a list of responsibilities other than just to keep his or her pet clean and fed. Because the animal is no longer in the wild—or never was part of a "wild" population—care must be taken not to adversely affect those remaining in the wild.

Record Keeping

Once you've glanced through this book, you'll be able to see why it's so important to keep good records. Records not only help you keep track of what you've done, they also enable you to *prove* what you've done. Record your reptile or amphibian's habits, what it eats, how often it eats, and when you breed it and the background of its mate. The genetics behind developing and maintaining color and pattern morphs can be amazingly detailed. Should your animals produce a really extraordinary clutch, you'll want to be able to repeat this sort of success.

Responsibility

One fact you need to remember when you're dealing with color and pattern morphs is that you're dealing with a largely artificial animal. Reptiles and amphibians in their natural coloration

Albino Nile monitor, courtesy of Ben Seigel.

and patterns have a hard enough time living long enough to reproduce. Those saddled with unnatural colors or patterns are incredibly visible when released into the wild. Don't do it—if only for humane reasons.

Survival

Captive snakes don't have to work very hard to survive. Some, like the majority of corn snakes, are the product of generation upon generation of captive-breeding. There has been no selection for skill at finding food, or for breeding to the biggest and strongest male, or for evading capture. These animals are going to have a very difficult time just finding food.

Gene Pool Contamination

Another very strong reason not to release animals into the wild is that the natural gene pools can get contaminated. The rosy boas in our southwestern states have been isolated so long in their canyon homes that their patterns are canyon-specific. This is evolution in its classic form. A few sloppy actions can destroy the results

of hundreds of years of evolution and isolation for any species.

By the process of seeking out an unusual color or pattern, you have assumed responsibility for the animal. If you cannot keep it, and cannot find a dependable adoptive home for it, have the animal humanely euthanized.

Reptiles, Amphibians, and the Law

There are many laws that regulate the collection from the wild, transportation of, and even the keeping of reptiles and amphibians. Since laws change regularly, vary by state and sometimes by city, and involve several federal agencies as well, it is not our intent to try to give you comprehensive information here. We merely want to make you aware of the fact that laws *do* exist.

An ever-increasing number of states prohibit the commercialization of, and occasionally the

Herpetoculturists selectively breed Amazon tree boas, **Corallus hortulanus hortulanus,** *to achieve brighter reds and yellows.*

keeping of, indigenous reptiles and amphibians without a permit or license. Some states make exceptions for designer colors. For example, Florida does not allow commercialization of normal phase Florida pinesnakes, but does allow commercialization of the albino phase only.

Most states consider some of their rarer herpetofauna threatened or endangered. Permits are necessary to collect, keep, or in some cases even to photograph these species.

Federal Laws and Regulations

Federal laws regulate the international or interstate commerce and transportation of federally threatened, endangered, or state-protected wildlife. Become familiar with all existing laws.

CHECKLIST

Laws

1 It is illegal to ship turtles and snakes via the United States Postal Service.

2 It is illegal to sell turtles having a shell length of less than 4 inches (10 cm). This is governed by the United States Public Health Service.

3 A growing number of municipalities, and some states, are legislating against the keeping of giant snakes, venomous herps, crocodilians, and giant lizards. In some cases species as common as green iguanas are included in these bans. Check the laws carefully before acquiring possibly problematic species. Comply, don't violate!

To learn of the various federal laws and regulations, including interstate transportation and commerce of herps collected in violation of state laws, check with the nearest office of the United States Fish and Wildlife Service. Penalties for violation are severe. Research and comply.

The non-game division of your state's Department of Fish and Wildlife, also called Department of Conservation, will be able to advise you of laws and regulations applicable at state level.

Your city or county commission can advise you of local regulations, ordinances, or laws.

As a keeper of reptiles or amphibians, it is your responsibility to learn about and comply with all existing laws and regulations. Occasionally,

Albino yellow rat snakes, **Elaphe obsoleta quadrivittata,** *are well established in herpetoculture.*

permits allowing you to keep a species that is otherwise prohibited may be available. The time to learn all of the complexities pertaining to the hobby of herpetoculture is prior to, not subsequent to, acquisition.

At least two forms of albinism occur in the black rat snake. This example is tyrosinase positive.

THE GENETICS OF COLOR MORPHS

When offering possible identifications of reptiles and amphibians, field guides rely heavily on color and pattern. But if you were to walk into a reptile and amphibian (herp) expo with a field guide and the intent of identifying something as common as a corn snake, you just might be stymied.

Corn Snakes

Today, rather than just the variable reds mentioned in field guides, corn snakes come in shades of orange, yellow, gray, mocha, lavender, and cream. Instead of being patterned only in a regular series of black-edged darker red saddles, as they once were, corn snakes with stripes, either straight or zigzag, narrow blotches, wide blotches, half-blotched and half-striped, round spots, haphazard patches of pigment, calicoes, and other variations have been developed.

In fact, among hobbyists, corn snakes are often referred to as the guppy of the snake world. Like the short-tailed, normally finned, wild guppy, the original corn snake color and pattern have been largely left by the wayside, being outshown by their variants.

Now being bred by Bob Mailloux at his Sandfire Dragon Ranch, albino green treefrogs, Hyla cinerea, are one of the newest additions to the American pet scene.

Other Snakes

Nor are corn snakes alone in their plethora of designer colors, although they *are* unquestionably the most variable. Designer colors and patterns are now the norm with California kingsnakes, Ruthven's kingsnakes, Honduran milksnakes, yellow rat snakes, black rat snakes, Texas rat snakes, ball pythons, Burmese pythons, common boa constrictors, and several species of garter snakes. One or two aberrant colors of many other species and subspecies have been developed and stabilized.

Lizards, Turtles, Geckos, and Sliders

Among the lizards and turtles, leopard geckos, fat-tailed geckos, and red-eared sliders display a hodgepodge of colors and patterns. Even crocodilians are known to occur in leucistic morphs.

Amphibians

Amphibians haven't been worked with as intensively as the reptiles by herpetoculturists,

but even among these there are many color variants of several horned frog species and of the aquatic salamander known as the axolotl, as well as a lesser number of variants of African clawed (underwater) frogs, American bullfrogs, southern leopard frogs, and dumpy (White's) treefrogs.

Beside color and pattern aberrancies, hobbyists are, much to the chagrin of conservationists and systematists who are worried about

SerpenCo produces some of the prettiest butter corn snakes.

escaped or released examples surviving to pollute gene pools, busily hybridizing and intergrading species and subspecies. A kingsnake-rat snake cross? Certainly, we have that; would you like the albino form?

Where will all of this stop? The chances are that it won't. We don't even pretend to know what the next big breakthrough in genetic manipulation will be, but as hobbyist interest grows, so, too, will the list of designer reptiles and amphibians.

Now we invite you to travel with us as in the following pages we glance at what was first thought to be merely a fleeting fad, but what has now come to be recognized for what it truly is—the continuing odyssey in the wonderful and ever-broadening world of designer reptiles and amphibians.

Understanding Selective Breeding

Linebreeding

Selective breeding (linebreeding) of a reptile or amphibian is not necessarily always in pursuit of albinism, unusual pattern, or other aberrant characteristic. Rather, it can be a sustained effort to merely assure that certain desired traits remain stabilized. A typical example is the Okeetee corn snake. The intense coloration and

This pastel scarlet kingsnake,
Lampropeltis triangulum elapsoides,
pictured with a normal phase, was found in southwest Florida.

Helpful Terms to Know

Aberrant—as used herein, not of normal appearance

Albino—deficient in black pigment

Allele—as used herein, either one of the two paired genes causing an inherited color or pattern

Amelanistic—lacking black pigment

Anerythristic—lacking red pigment

Axanthic—deficient in yellow pigment

Chromatophore—pigment cell

Codominant—having two equally dominant characteristics

Dichromatism—differing base colors within the same species

Dimorphism—differing characteristics (size or color) within the same species; may be sex-linked

Dominant—as used herein, an allele that causes a specific characteristic

Embryogenesis—the ongoing development of an embryo

Erythristic—as used herein, having excessive red pigment

Erythrophore—a red chromatophore

Heterozygous—having recessive traits because of differing gene pairs

Homozygous—having dominant traits because of identical gene pairs

Hypomelanistic—being deficient in melanin

Hypopigmentation—having reduced pigmentation

Leucistic—white (this is different than albinism or amelanism)

Linebreeding—selectively breeding for a specific trait

Melanistic—darker than normal in color (not necessarily black) due to increased amounts of melanin

Melanophore—as used herein, a melanin-producing chromatophore

Morph—a visible characteristic

Mutation—as used herein, a visibly different characteristic (color, pattern, or appearance)

Phenotype—identifying external characteristics

Piebald—having abnormal areas of contrasting pigment

Polymorphic—having more than a single morph (as in color or pattern)

Recessive—as used herein, having non-identical alleles capable of causing a specific trait only when paired

Synthesize—as used herein, having the ability to produce pigments and enzymes

Tyrosinase—the enzyme allowing synthesis of melanin

Tyrosinase negative—lacking tyrosinase

Tyrosinase positive—having tyrosinase yet incapable of synthesizing melanin

Xanthic—yellow(ish)

Xanthophore—a pigment cell allowing the synthesizing of red, yellow, or intermediate pigments

definitive markings of the Okeetee phase corn snake—a naturally occurring color phase—has long made it a hobbyist favorite. Hobbyists linebreed tiger rat snakes—the naturally very yellow Mexican form—in an effort to retain, or even enhance, the amount of yellows and oranges present. There isn't any concerted work being done to develop an albino (although that would be nice), merely to enhance and stabilize desirable qualities already present.

It is likely that the genes causing albinism differ on these two Taiwan beauty snakes,
Elaphe taeniura freesi. *The pale individual (left) may be tyrosinase negative while the
more richly colored individual is thought to be t positive.*

Linebreeding involves breeding together the most brilliant male and female, then breeding father with daughter, mother with son, or the pair with the most desirable patterns, and doing this over and over, upgrading and diversifying the gene pool whenever possible. It may take generations of effort to develop and stabilize a given trait, or you may be lucky and have a significant breakthrough occur in only a generation or two.

The progeny of any given union may look like either or both of the parents, but may occasionally be of very different appearance.

As you selectively breed your reptiles or amphibians you should be aware of two primary terms, *heterozygous* and *homozygous*.

Defined, homozygous means having two identical alleles for a given trait and heterozygous means having nonidentical alleles for that given trait. In everyday parlance, this would mean that homozygous herps breed true for a given trait, but that the trait is present, but masked, in heterozygous specimens.

A Breeding Project Example

Let's take a look at a breeding project with the California kingsnake as an example.

When you breed two normal or two albino Cal kings together (we'll ignore the tyrosinase factor for this example), the resulting offspring are usually similar in appearance to the parents. That's fairly straightforward.

But then you start out with an adult normally colored female and an adult albino male. The snakes breed and you think "Wow— albino babies!" The eggs incubate successfully, but when they hatch, all—every last one—are the normal color of the female. What has happened? (Check Punnet Square number 1 on page 17.)

	A	A
a	aA	aA
a	aA	aA

In reality everything is absolutely normal, exactly the way it should be. The babies that you have just hatched, called the F1 generation, look normally colored, but they are each heterozygous for albinism. They have one gene for albinism, and one for normal coloration. The normal coloration gene masks or is dominant over the albino gene. If you breed one of the female babies back with the albino male, statistically the clutch should (and probably will) contain 50 percent albinos and 50 percent normally colored hatchlings (see Punnet Square number 2 below). There are two phenotypes resulting from this breeding, the aa and the aA.

	a	A
a	aa	aA
a	aa	aA

But what happens if you breed a heterozygous baby to a sibling of the opposite sex?

Statistically, the clutch from such a union will contain 25 percent albinos, 25 percent normals, and 50 percent heterozygous babies that are of normal coloration. That's three phenotypes. Except through breeding trials, it is impossible for a hobbyist to ascertain which of the 75 percent of the normally colored babies are fully normal and which are heterozygous (see Punnet Square number 3 below).

	a	A
a	aa	aA
A	aA	AA

These are the everyday genetics of simple dominant and recessive traits. But things aren't always that easy. Sometimes two different alleles result in young that look like both parents. Paul Hollander, a geneticist at Iowa State University, was kind enough to explain how this works. In a case like this, if a red flower is fertilized with a white flower, the first generation, or the F1 generation, is all pink. When you self-fertilize the pinks, you get 25 percent red, 50 percent pink, and 25 percent white. If you self-fertilize the red plants, you get all red offspring; if you self-fertilize the whites, you get all white offspring. There are three phenotypes at work here, red, white, and pink (the newer form of writing alleles is to use one letter with a superscript for the normal allele, so an albino would be a, the normal a^+): red is WW, white is W^+W^+, and pink is WW^+. This is called *codominance*, and as Paul Hollander says, you can easily tell what the heterozygote is.

Codominance appears in some snake species. The tiger reticulated python is one of them. The homozygous tiger, called the super tiger, when bred to the homozygous normal reticulated

The silver morph of the Trans-Pecos rat snake is now gaining in popularity.

TIP

Albinism

It was once thought that albinism involved a total lack of pigmentation and that albino organisms necessarily had pink irises and a dark-red pupil. As now understood, albinism is simply a deficiency, but not necessarily a total lack of pigmentation. The animal is of lighter (usually much lighter) than normal coloration, may be somewhat translucent, especially as a baby, and may have either blue or pink irises and dark-red pupils. Reference is often made by herpeticulturists breeding corn snakes to red albinos and white albinos, the differentiation being the intensity of the red coloration displayed.

---

python, results in the heterozygous tiger, which is intermediate in appearance between the two. There are three genotypes and three phenotypes. Very direct. Be aware that terminology for this sort of phenomenon is not yet nailed down, and that you may also hear terms such as "incomplete dominant" or "partial dominant." For reptile and amphibian breeding, the term *codominance* is well enough accepted to avoid confusion.

Multiple Traits

With the number of variants now available in many species, these examples are the mere tip of a very big genetic iceberg. Some herps may be heterozygous for two or more traits, and spontaneous color and pattern aberrations seem to turn up annually.

For a striped Cal king that is also albino, bred to a normal Cal king female (again, we're ignoring the tyrosinase factor), striped is represented by capital S; normal pattern is represented by a lowercase s.

Note: Striped is dominant in Cal kings.

	aS	as
As	AaSs	Aass
As	AaSs	Aass

This yields 50 percent normal striped and 50 percent normal banded.

About Tyrosinase

There are certainly several genes that contribute to albinism, and the gene that controls tyrosinase production is one of them. Tyrosinase is produced in melanophores, the cells that produce black and brown pigments. The melanophores use tyrosinase, a copper-containing enzyme, and import tyrosine, an amino acid, to create melanin. No tyrosinase means no melanism. If an animal cannot produce tyrosinase, it is said to be tyrosinase negative, a type of albinism.

But a tyrosinase-positive animal is also a type of albino. In this case the melanophore can produce tyrosinase, but either it cannot import the tyrosine, or there's a blockage, as yet unknown, that prevents the tyrosinase from acting on the tyrosine. Both the tyrosinase-positive (t+) and the tyrosinase-negative (t–) types can also have other mutations that contribute to their degree and type of albinisim. (We do not yet know enough about albinism in amphibians to even speculate about possible types of albinism.)

You can often look at an albino reptile and make a good guess about the tyrosinanse + or –. The colors displayed tend to be less

Brilliant orange as hatchlings, as they age, hypomelanistic Florida kingsnakes, **Lampropeltis getula floridana,** *fade to pale yellow.*

contrasting in the t-negative specimens. When a t-negative specimen is bred to a t-positive specimen, the resulting offspring are *normally* colored, but are doubly heterozygous (heterozygous for both factors). This means that a percentage of albino babies will be produced whether the specimen is bred to a t-negative or a t-positive partner. If you want to be certain about the tyrosinase-positive or -negative quality of a reptile, you'll need to submit a fresh piece of the animal's skin for what's called a *dopa reaction.* The skin is incubated for a specified length of time in a solution of dopa. If tyrosinase is present (tyrosinase positive), it reacts with the dopa and the melanophores turn dark due to the melanin they have produced.

Amelanism

The condition known as amelanism (meaning literally "without black," a form of albinism) is characterized by a total lack of melanin. This is the term now used by hobbyists to describe red-eyed whitish reptiles of many species and lineages. The terminology is most often heard when hobbyists discuss corn snakes.

Anerythrism

Anerythrism is a term used by hobbyists to describe the lack of red pigment in corn and other predominantly red snakes. Since a single

type of color-containing cell, the xanthophore, is responsible for both red and yellow pigmentation, the phenomenon is the same as axanthism (literally "without yellow").

Hypomelanism

Hypomelanism is a variable and often naturally occurring reduction of dark pigment (hypo means "reduced"). Hypomelanistic individuals of many snake species are now commonly bred by many hobbyists and are often seen in the pet trade.

Carl May owned and photographed this piebald brown house snake, **Lamprophis fuliginosus.**

Scalelessness is known to occur in several snake species. Pictured is a Texas rat snake bred by Dr. Bern Bechtel, who has long researched the genetics of reptiles and amphibians.

TIP

Scales

A snake has scales, right?

Not always!

The phenomenon of scalelessness is now well documented in western diamond-backed rattlesnakes, Texas rat snakes, and more rarely in other snake taxa. These snakes are essentially smooth-skinned snakes, but there is a price to pay, as far as the snake is concerned. Because there are no scales to support and contour their jaws, scaleless snakes often have malformed snouts and jawlines.

Leucism

Although it is well documented in other species, leucism in reptiles is perhaps best known in the Texas rat snake and the American alligator. It is also well known in both the African clawed frog and the axolotl. Because in leucism all chromatophores of all colors are defective, leucistic herps are pure white, lacking pattern, but have dark, often blue, eyes. Occasionally, patches of dark coloration may appear with age, giving the animal a piebald appearance.

Melanism

Melanism is the term used to define an excess of dark pigmentation caused by the pigment melanin. Reptiles and amphibians may be abnormally dark from birth (Mexican black kingsnake), or melanistic tendencies may occur during normal ontogenetic changes.

Many reptiles, and some amphibians, undergo natural age-related color changes, some of which can be dramatic. Three examples of ontogenetic changes occur in the yellow rat snake, the black milksnake, and the red-eared slider. Hatchlings of the first are a strongly blotched, tannish brown, while the adults are prominently striped and decidedly yellow in coloration. A black milksnake begins life as a black-, white-, and red-ringed baby, but with age becomes suffused with pattern- and color-obliterating black pigment. Likewise, male red-eared sliders, which have a forest-green carapace as babies, become so suffused with melanin that characteristic markings are all but obscured.

However, not all incidences of dark coloration are caused by an actual excess of melanin. In some instances the predominating dark coloration may be due to the suppression of a companion color. Such is the case with

This herpetocultural oddity is a hybrid between two kingsnake species, the gray-banded and the Arizona mountain (Lampropeltis alterna and L. pyromelana ssp., respectively).

anerythristic corn snakes. Anerythristic examples of this beautiful snake are predominantly deep brown due to the lack of red pigmentation.

Piebald

Herps that bear abnormal blotching or patching, often of white, but occasionally of other colors, are called piebald. This condition, only recently determined to be genetically replicable, is now seen in ball pythons, corn snakes, eastern garter snakes, and African clawed frogs.

Pattern

Pattern anomalies are now as commonplace in captive-bred snakes as are aberrant colors. They are less well documented in other reptile groups and in amphibians. Normally banded or blotched snakes of many species and sub-species (corn snakes, Great Plains rat snakes, Honduran milksnakes) are now readily available in striped or unicolored phases.

Color Changes

Some color changes may be dramatic and change with the time of day. Brazilian rainbow boas, often quite a bright orange by day, may become overlain with a silvery sheen at night. Many frogs are also colored differently by day and night. One, the Amazonian spotted treefrog, is yellow-spotted green by day and a russet at night.

Hybrids

Although almost unheard of in the wild, captive-breedings of multigeneric hybrids are not at all uncommon. This is especially true in the world of snakes, where hobbyists are now routinely interbreeding gopher snakes *(Pituophis)* with rat snakes *(Elaphe)*.

A multispecific hybrid results from the successful breeding of two species within the same genus. An example would be a corn snake *(Elaphe guttata guttata)* breeding with a yellow rat snake *(Elaphe obsoleta quadrivittata)*.

Intraspecific hybrids occur when two non-contiguous races of a single species successfully interbreed. An example of this would be a black milksnake *(Lampropeltis triangulum gaigeae)* breeding with a Mexican milksnake *(L. t. annulata)*—the two races are separated by several other subspecies.

Intergrades

An intergrade is the result of the successful breeding of two contiguous subspecies of reptiles. The young are usually intermediate in appearance between the two parent races. Example: yellow rat snake *(E. o. quadrivittata)*, black rat snake *(E. o. obsoleta)*.

Color, Scale, and Pattern Anomalies

Color and pattern anomalies, as well as other characteristics, in reptiles—we don't yet know about amphibians—can be caused not only by genetics, but by external stimuli as well.

TDSD

The sex of some oviparous (egg-laying) reptiles can be determined by the incubation temperature. This is referred to as temperature-dependent sex determination. When females of some live-bearing snakes, such as common boas, are kept very warm, the babies produced are often striped rather than saddled.

With many species of turtles, abnormally high nest temperatures produce females, and abnormally low nest temperatures produce males. A suitably ambient temperature, which can vary by species but which is usually in the low to mid-80s°F (27–29°C), will allow both sexes to develop. It is possible that during a

Albinism is coveted by hobbyists. This albino fat-tailed gecko, Hemitheconyx caudicinctus, *is owned by The Gourmet Rodent.*

normal incubation, eggs near the top of the nest, which are more quickly warmed to higher temperatures by the sun, will produce female turtles, while the cooler ones on the bottom of the nest will produce males.

The opposite is true with many lizards, but with an additional twist. Females are produced at cooler temeperatures and males at warmer temperatures, but then females, often with an aggressive male-like disposition, will be produced at very hot temperatures.

Deformities

Excessively high or low incubation temperatures can produce shell-scute deformities in turtles. Shell plates may be either divided to produce a high number or, more rarely, undivided and fewer than normal in number.

Color of Turtles

The color of some baby turtles can also be affected by abnormal nest temperatures. For example, rather than being clad in carapacial scutes of their normal dark-marked green coloration, hatchling red-eared sliders incubated at high temperatures are often pastel green, tan, or even blue-green in coloration and may have substantially more red on their head than those incubated at normal temperatures.

Color of Lizards

It is not known with certainty that abnormal incubation temperatures affect the color of lizards, but this is a possibility. On the other hand, when eggs are improperly incubated, or when gestating females of viviparous species are kept at unsuitable temperatures, spinal and other skeletal deformities are well documented.

Sex Determination

It is thought that sex determination in all snakes is genetic rather than temperature induced. However, when developing embryos are subjected to unsuitable temperatures, pattern and skeletal aberrancies have been noted. Striped individuals of the common boa, a species normally having well-defined saddles, are often produced by females kept marginally too warm, and some hatchling milksnakes may have fewer or more rings than normal. Although the pattern aberrancies may be welcomed, on the downside, there is the possibility of the before-mentioned moderate to severe skeletal deformities.

Scales

In simple terms, a reptile's scale is comprised of folds of skin that begin developing early in embryogenesis. It is not known what phenomenon causes the failure of the scales to develop, but this phenomenon has been noted in some species of rat snakes, kingsnakes, bullsnakes, garter snakes, and rattlesnakes.

Scalelessness seems not to affect the viability of the snakes affected, but shedding problems may occur.

One of the most bizarre of the physical anomalies seen in snakes is a partial to complete lack of dorsal and lateral scales. The ventral scales are usually present but are often abnormal. There is also a report of a rattlesnake having its scales reversed in orientation.

Clive Longden specializes in breeding albino turtles. Pictured is an albino western painted turtle, **Chrysemys picta bellii.**

Although red eyes are present on this juvenile Nile monitor, **Varanus niloticus ssp.,** *which is owned by Ben Seigel, albinism can be present even when the eyes are dark.*

OBTAINING YOUR DESIGNER REPTILES AND AMPHIBIANS

Although some designer reptiles and amphibians are so abundant and inexpensive now that they are available in pet stores, many are still costly and only sporadically available. The high-end species—designer ball pythons, some newly developed corn snakes, albino snapping turtles, and so on—are often available only from specialty dealers, at captive-breeder expos, or from the breeders themselves. Let's explore some of these avenues of acquisition.

Pet Stores

Look in pet stores for species such as albino horned frogs, designer leopard geckos, albino corn snakes, or albino clawed frogs. All are inexpensive and hardy. We advocate pet store acquisitions whenever possible because of their convenience and the ability of the customer to discuss the species in which they are interested with a knowledgeable store employee. Such things as routine care are easily covered, but your pet store cannot be expected to know the

Matt Lerer posed and photographed this blue example of the painted-bellied monkey frog, Phyllomedusa sauvagei.

history and genetics of either normal-appearing or designer specimens that are captive-bred. There are times when, despite their efforts to provide accurate information, your pet store employee might err. In the store's defense, the employee may just be repeating information given by the supplier. Remember, your local pet shop is often two or even three or four times removed from the initial dealing that placed the specimen in the pet trade.

Unfortunately, information given, whether accurate or erroneous, is often self-perpetuating. When giving information to a new hobbyist, it would benefit all if conversations started out with a qualifying statement such as, "Our

The term "sockhead" has been coined by herpetoculturists to describe a snake with an abnormally black head and neck. This is a desert kingsnake, **Lampropeltis getula splendida**.

supplier tells us . . ." and ends with another qualifier such as, "This may, or may not, be accurate. I'd suggest you try to corroborate this."

Expos

Reptile and amphibian (herp) expos are now held in many larger cities across the United States and are becoming popular in Europe. It seems that there is at least one occurring at some point in the United States on any given weekend. Some are annual events; others may be biannual or quarterly. An expo is merely a gathering of dealers and breeders, all under one roof. They vary in size from the 500+ tables of the National Reptile Breeders' Expo, which is held in Florida every August, to some having only 25 to 50 tables. Your best selection of both common and rare designer herps will probably be at this kind of gathering. Reptile and amphibian hobbyist magazines usually carry the dates and locations of expos across the United States (see Information, page 92).

Breeders

Breeders of designer herps may vary in size from hobbyists who produce only a few individuals of one or two species to commercial breeders who produce literally thousands of hatchlings of numerous kinds each season. With each passing year, more and more breeders present the fruits of their labors at herp expos, but there are many who do not. Many can be found advertising in the classified or pictorial ads sections in specialty reptile and amphibian magazines (see the Special Interest Group section, page 92). Breeders usually offer parasite-free, well-acclimated specimens and accurate information. Most keep records of genetics, lineage, fecundity, health, and quirks of the species with which they work, and especially of the specimens in their breeding programs.

Most breeders of designer herps selectively breed for both new and enhanced colors and patterns.

Specialty Dealers

The continuing growth in popularity of reptiles and amphibians has allowed specialty dealers to spring up. Besides often breeding fair numbers of the reptiles they offer, specialty dealers deal directly with other breeders across the world and may even be direct importers. Imported specimens are usually acclimated, and have been fed and, often, subjected to a veterinary checkup. Many such dealers buy and sell reptiles and amphibians at herp expos as well as advertise in reptile and amphibian magazines.

Mail-order Purchase and Shipping

Once you've researched the subject and decided on the type of designer herp you want, how do you go about actually finding and acquiring it?

There are actually several ways to do so. Among these are

World Wide Web: By instructing your search engine to seek the species in which you are interested you should learn of several hundred breeders, many of whom have excellent photos on their web site.

Classified ads: Dealers and hobbyists list their available livestock in the classified ads of the several reptile and amphibian, and pet, magazines.

Word of mouth: Ask friends and fellow enthusiasts for recommendations about the reptile dealers they know of. Try to check their reliability by asking about the dealers at nature centers, museums, zoos, or among hobbyist groups.

Once You've Decided . . .

What next? Now that you've found the designer herp you decided on earlier and you have learned that your potential supplier has a satisfactory reputation, it is time to contact the vendor to finalize details.

Shipping Information

What is involved with shipping? The shipping of reptiles is not at all the insurmountable barrier that many hobbyists initially think it will be, but it can add substantially to the cost of your

As seen in this Peninsula kingsnake, **Lampropeltis getula** *ssp., anerythrism produces a black and white coloration rather than the typical brown and yellow.*

The unusually narrow red bands of this albino Sinaloan milksnake, **Lampropeltis triangulum sinaloae,** *suggest that it has been hybridized with a milksnake of another race.*

This albino western cottonmouth, **Agkistrodon piscivorous leucostoma,** *owned by Chris McQuade, is inordinately defensive.*

chosen herp. The chances are excellent that your vendor is quite familiar with shipping and will be delighted to assist you in any way possible.

Among the things on which you and your shipper will have to agree is the method of payment and the method and date of shipping.

Payment

Some vendors will collect the cost of shipping from you, then prepay the charges. This can help expedite the transaction. Unless the shipper knows you well, he or she will almost always insist that the specimen (including boxing charges and shipping if applicable) be paid for in full prior to shipment being made. If you are in a hurry for the specimen, it will probably be necessary to get a money order or cashier's check to the shipper, or to supply the shipper with a credit card number or wire transfer of

funds to his or her account. Many shippers will accept personal checks but will not ship until the check has cleared their bank, usually a week or so after deposit.

An alternate method of payment is COD; however, this can be expensive and inconvenient. Most airlines will accept cash only for the COD amount and there is a hefty COD surcharge (upward of $15) in addition to all other charges.

Methods of Shipping

There are now many options available for shipping herps.

✔ Amphibians and lizards can be shipped via express mail, but the United States Postal Service will not accept snakes or turtles. All herps can now be shipped by services such as Airborne or FedEx, or by air freight.

This albino Texas coral snake, **Micrurus tener,** *photographed by Mike Price, is owned by Ryan Blakely.*

✔ The door to-door-services (Airborne, FedEx, Express Mail) are less expensive and far more convenient than air freight. These services cost between $15 and $40. It will be necessary for someone to be at home to sign for the package on any of the door-to-door services.

✔ Air freight is an airport-to-airport service. There are usually either two or three levels of service available. Charges may vary dramatically by airline, so plan your shipment, including the level of service you wish to use, carefully.

✔ Regular, space available freight can cost as little as $35. Guaranteed flights may be more than twice that cost. Your vendor will quite likely suggest the best and least expensive service for your transaction.

Ship only during "good" weather and understand that your animals will run a risk of being delayed if weather conditions are adverse or during the peak holiday travel/shipping/mailing times.

Unless otherwise specified, reliable shippers guarantee live delivery; however, to substantiate the existence of a problem, both shippers and shipping companies may require a "discrepancy" or "damage" report made out, signed, and dated by shipping company personnel. In the very rare case when a problem occurs, contact your shipper immediately for instructions.

Soon you will no longer find the shipping of specimens intimidating. Understanding the system will open wide new doors of acquisition.

BOAS AND PYTHONS

It was not so many years ago that aberrant boid snakes—designer colors of the boas and pythons—were considered luxury items affordable to only the wealthiest of herpetoculturists. Albinos and other odd colors of all boids sold for thousands of dollars each. Because many species are prolific and comparatively easy to breed, their prices have dropped from several thousand dollars each to only about $50. This speaks volumes about the success of modern-day herpetoculture.

Not all boids, whether of normal or aberrant color, have found favor with hobbyists. For example, although albino green anacondas, *Eunectes murinus* (the world's heaviest snake), have been developed, they are seldom seen in collections. Adult females can exceed 20 feet (6 m)! Although adults of the blood python, *Python curtus* ssp., reach only 7–9 feet (2.1–2.7 m) in length, they are also of immense girth. The species is only moderately popular with hobbyists. Albinism has occurred in this species, and albino hatchlings are occasionally available to hobbyists. Albinos have peachy-red markings against a lighter ground color.

Prohibitively costly only two decades ago, today baby albino Burmese pythons are hardly more expensive than those of normal coloration. An adult female can exceed 20 feet in length.

Types of Pythons

The Burmese Python

However, at the other extreme, the Burmese python, *Python molurus bivitattus*, became one of the most popular snakes in today's market, despite the fact that it is not fully suited to be a "pet" snake.

The Burmese python is one of five of the world's largest snake species. Females, the larger sex, may exceed 20 feet (6 m) in length. When normally colored, this immensely powerful constrictor is tan with large dark brown dorsal saddles. In the 1980s albinism was introduced into a breeding program. From that, as well as from some subsequent spontaneous additional aberrancies, come the multitude of colors and patterns available today.

Because of their strength and immediate feeding responses, large Burmese pythons can

Disposing of Specimens

Do keep in mind that it is not usually easy to dispose of a large specimen of any giant snake. Zoos, museums, nature centers, and most breeders will not accept these unwanted pet snakes.

be dangerous snakes. Sadly, it seems as if a hobbyist is killed by a "pet" Burmese every year or two. Because of this, as well as because of the general public's fear of snakes, many communities now legislate against the keeping of giant snakes. Before acquiring one, ascertain whether your community allows you to keep a Burmese (or any other large snake). Obey the law!

As hobbyists hone their breeding programs, new and exciting patterns and colors of Burmese pythons, Python molurus bivitattus, *such as these labyrinth patterned babies, continue to appear.*

Although baby Burmese pythons are easily kept and fed, larger ones become increasingly problematic. Within two years the snake can be nearly 15 feet in length, requires a strong, spacious cage (4 × 4 × 8 feet [1.2 × 1.2 × 2.4 m] minimum), eats adult rabbits, and is a real chore to handle and maintain. We strongly urge that you never work with a boa or python that is more than 8 feet (2.4 m) in length without having a second qualified person in attendance. No matter how tractable you feel your giant snake is, an accident with tragic consequences can take place in a heartbeat.

Albinism in Burmese Pythons

Albinism in the Burmese python has proven to be a simple recessive character, but, as with other albino snakes, there may be more than a single gene. At hatching, one of the phases has lavender saddles on a white background. Although popularly referred to as tyrosinase positive, at this time the designations are speculative. When the babies are white with a pink pattern they are popularly referred to as tyrosinase negative, again speculative. With age the colors become a little richer, the white becoming creamier, and the pinks and lavenders yellower.

Albinism has also been incorporated into a green (patternless) morph and into both the labyrinth and granite color phase.

Green Burmese

The green Burmese is an interesting army-green snake that has a dark dorsal pattern of linear stripes and spots when small. The pattern fades with age, and many older individuals are a solid patternless green. The granite morph has the dark dorsal blotches fragmented into an irregular and very busy pattern. Granite and green phases

Cheryl Bott is sizing these beautifully patterned tiger morph reticulated pythons, **Python reticulatus,** *for breeding.*

have been combined and the (probably codominant) result is a green Burmese with patches of granite pattern. The labyrinth pattern consists of a less fragmented dorsal pattern and the spots and stripes have less-irregular edges.

Blonde Burmese

The blonde Burm has a normal pattern but has yellowish rather than brown dorsal blotches and a very light ground color. It seems likely that this coloration will soon be selectively bred into other patterns.

Fading Pattern

The fading pattern is an interesting phenomenon. Hatchlings have a normal well-defined pattern but with growth, the dark markings begin to fade. There is a tendency for what pattern there is to be best defined anteriorly and to be especially so on the head.

A dark-eyed snow-white morph (leucistic) of the Burmese python has been found on at least two occasions. These have never been bred successfully; thus virtually nothing is known about the genetics behind the color.

Reticulated Python

The Asian-Malaysian reticulated python, *P. reticulatus*, is another of the giant snakes, at least in the majority of cases. It can attain or even exceed 25 feet (7.6 m) in length. Unlike the Burmese python, reticulated pythons are often irascible; however, before further decrying the keeping of this snake, we must state that some of the more recently available insular forms seem to be true dwarfs, seldom exceeding 8 feet (2.4 m) in length. Pattern and color aberrancies do not seem to have yet been recorded in these small morphs.

Thus, with the same admonitions that we presented for the Burmese python—whether you are truly set up to keep these giant snakes, whether they are legal in your area, and if so, whether you are prepared to never work with one in excess of 8 feet while alone – we will mention some of the designer colors and patterns now available in the reticulated python.

Perhaps the simplest of the traits bred for is the perpetuation of a yellow head. Retics having this also often have a degree of brighter than normal yellow in their otherwise normal body pattern. Pink-eyed albinos of at least two ground colors—white and lavender—are now available. These are beautiful snakes that become more richly colored as growth occurs. Piebald or brindle mutants are also occasionally seen but have not yet been reproduced in any numbers. Piebaldism is variable. In some examples the snake may be primarily white with variable splotches of olive or gold, or the reverse may be true, with the darker colors being dominant.

Striping: Various striping patterns are now commonplace on retics. Three of these are a simple striping, a tiger morph, and a super tiger. The tiger morphs are beautiful tan-on-brown snakes (they pale with age) on which the dorsal blotches are relatively elongate and wholly or partially split medially by dark striping. The split, lozenge-shaped halves may be offset from each other. Both dorsal and lateral blotches are strongly outlined with dark pigment. The pattern borne by the super tiger morph is even more linear. Many,

if not all, of the light dorsal blotches are connected, thus becoming dark-edged dorsal stripes. A dark vertebral stripe is present and the lateral pattern is also lineate.

African Rock Pythons

The African rock python, *P. sebae*, is a third very large—12 to 15 feet (3.6–4.6 m)—and often bad-dispositioned python species. (Check community regulations and your ability to safely maintain a giant snake before purchasing one.) Although not particularly popular with hobbyists, a striped morph and a patternless morph are now occasionally available in the pet trade.

Ball Pythons

African ball pythons: Because it is a small species—usually less than 5 feet (1.5 m)—the tropical African ball python, *P. regius*, is one of the best of the pet pythons. This prettily colored, heavy-bodied python is now selectively bred in a great number of color and pattern morphs. Since it has small numbers of large eggs, designer ball pythons hold their value longer than aberrant morphs of the larger and more prolific pythons.

Axanthic ball pythons: When they were first seen, axanthic ball pythons were referred to as black. Although it is true that the lack of yellow pigment makes this morph much darker than normal, the pattern is well

It is only within the last few years that piebaldism has been determined heritable. Pictured is a ball python.

Although albinos are beautiful, because of their large adult size (upward of 20 feet), a defensive reticulated python can be a life-threatening adversary.

defined and readily visible. Much darker ball pythons, now referred to as melanistic, have been developed.

Typically, ball pythons have an intricate pattern of light dorsal saddles and lateral blotches. Occasionally, the light blotches may coalesce into a gold stripe or, conversely, be replaced by the extension and coalescing of the black pigment from the sides. The result is a ball python with either a gold or black dorsal stripe. The clown morph has an irregularly edged, almost zigzag, black middorsal stripe. The light lateral markings are equally irregular and each contains one or more dark spots.

Albino and piebald ball pythons: Two of the most striking color morphs are the albino and the piebald ball pythons. The former is a beautiful white snake with the pattern represented in golden to butter yellow. The latter is a normally patterned and colored ball python with variable patches or rings of stark, unpatterned white. The caramel or lavender albino is just that—an albino that has a pale caramel-lavender coloration where the black would normally be.

Pattern anomalies are also being selectively perpetuated. Among others are the pin-striped, where the pattern is reduced to very thin lines, the spiderweb, a busy pattern of thin spidery lines, the jungle, which has a colorful black and yellow pattern, and the Angola morph. This latter produces a ball python very much like the related but rare Angolan python, *P. anchitae*, in appearance.

Snow phase ball pythons: Snow phase ball pythons, largely white with muted yellow contrast, have only recently made their appearance in the industry.

Australian carpet pythons: Australian carpet pythons, *Morelia spilota* ssp., are pythons of moderate size. The coastal race, *M. s. mcdowelli*, attains a hefty 12- to 14-foot (3.6–4.3-m) length but most other races top out at 8 feet (2.4 m). To date, only a handful of albino and reduced contrast babies have been hatched. None are readily available yet. However, hobbyists continue to attempt to brighten the yellow and black contrasts of the beautiful "jungle" carpet python, *M. s. cheynei*, and to enhance the complexity of the pattern by intergrading the jungle race with the diamond python, *M. s. spilota*.

Green tree pythons: The green tree python, *Morelia viridis*, is a spectacular, arboreal, leaf-green constrictor of northeastern Australia, New Guinea, and surrounding islands. It is adult at from 4.5 to about 6 feet (1.4–1.8 m) in length. Although it seems difficult to us to enhance an already remarkably beautiful snake, hobbyists are busily attempting to do so. Tree pythons are hatched as yellow, russet, or chocolate-colored babies. With growth,

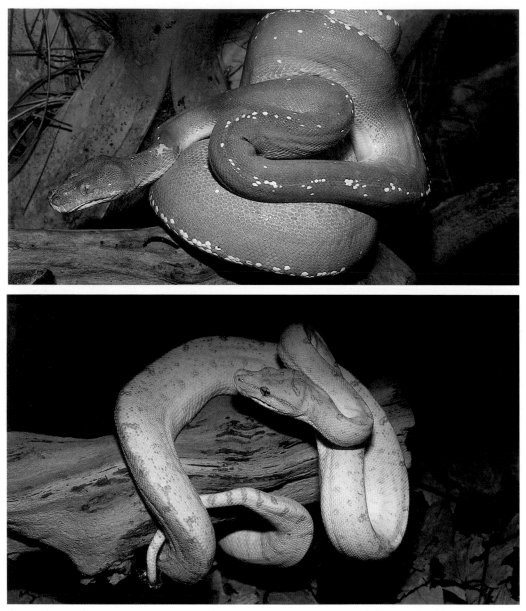

Normally leaf green, herpetoculturists are striving to stabilize both blue and yellow morphs of the green tree python, Morelia viridis.

a suffusion of blue modifies and transforms the snake into its green adult color; however, the blue occasionally fails to develop properly in some examples, allowing the yellow coloration to remain into adulthood. Conversely, the development of yellow is inhibited in other examples, producing a remarkable-appearing bluish snake. It is the blue and the yellow variants that herpetoculturists are striving to stabilize and perpetuate. Of course, should an albino appear during this intense selective breeding, it would find a ready market.

Types of Boas

Viper boas: Although they are not overly popular, both the viper boa, *Candoia asper*, of New Guinea, and the Solomon Islands ground boa, *C. carinata paulsoni*, have found favor with some hobbyists. Both of these snakes occur in a number of color phases that range from variable dark brown, through russet, to nearly white. Hobbyists seem more interested in perpetuating the whitest morphs. These are heavy-bodied constrictors that are adult at from 1.5 to 4 feet (.46–1.2 m) in length.

Kenyan sand boas: The Kenyan sand boa, *Eryx colubrinus loveridgei*, is a pretty orange and tan snake of eastern and southern Africa. The females are considerably larger than the males. As is suggested by its common name, this is a species of arid- and semiarid-land habitats and it is a persistent burrower. They have proven one of the easier species of the genus to breed in captivity. During the 1990s several designer morphs were developed. Among these are albino, anerythristic, and snow morphs.

The albinos are, of course, white snakes with rather well-defined yellowish markings. Because they lack red pigment, the anerythristic morph is black on gray, and the snow morph is white with very muted brighter markings.

Rosy boas: In the canyonlands and boulderfields of the southwestern United States and Mexico we have a small species of boa that is also adept at burrowing, but is often found beneath rocks and boulders in its semiarid-land habitat. This is the rosy boa, *Lichanura trivirgata* ssp. There are three subspecies, with true designer colors being largely restricted to one, the coastal rosy boa, *L. t. roseofusca*. Albinos of the coastal rosy boa, which are seen in two forms, red-eyed and dark-eyed, have been found and selective breeding programs for both are firmly established. In both cases, these snakes bear peachy orange markings on a pale tan to whitish ground color. Rosy boas have rather small clutches of fairly large babies, and if kept dry and warm, are among the hardiest of snakes.

Besides these designer colors, hobbyists linebreed the desert phase of the rosy boa, *L. t. gracia*, for particular color characteristics. In most cases these programs are aimed at perpetuating the genetic lineage of rosy boas from particular canyons.

Amazon tree boas: The next two species of boas hail from the neotropics. One, the 6-foot-long (1.8 m) but very slender Amazon tree boa, *Corallus hortulana hortulana*, is naturally variable, and it has some of the more brilliant ground colors that herpetoculturists strive to perpetuate. Among these are the brightest yellows and reds, naturally occurring colors that are diametrically opposed to the olives and grays usually associated with this arboreal boa. Although some tree boas are reasonably tractable, many are very defensive and will readily bite the hand that intends to feed them.

Boa Constrictor

The various races of the boa constrictor, *Boa constrictor* ssp., are exceeded by New World snakes in size only by the gigantic anacondas. Boas have been available in the pet industry for at least 55 years, but it is only in the last 20 years that they have been captive-bred with any regularity or that designer colors and patterns have been available. These live-bearing snakes are still considered by many herpetoculturists to be far less reliable breeders than most of the pythons.

Although an albino red-tailed boa, *B. c. constrictor*, has recently been found, it has not yet been bred in captivity. Providing it survives and can be successfully cycled reproductively, albino red-tailed boas should appear in the pet hobby within the next few years. However, after several false starts, albinism is now well established in the common (or Colombian) boa constrictor, *B. c. imperator*. This is the last of the boas that we will discuss in detail. Besides albinism, striping and a salmon morph are the subject of current breeding projects.

Typically, boas are tan or creamy brown to gray (darkest at the northern and southern extremes of the range) with darker crossbands and some degree of dorsolateral striping. On the posterior quarter of the body and the tail, the ground color intensifies to red or maroon. The boas with the reddest tails occur in the Amazonian rain forests.

Mocha boas: Very occasionally, a boa may be devoid or largely devoid of all markings. One such, recently acquired by California Zoological Supply, has been dubbed the "mocha" boa.

Paradox boas: Albinism, of course, replaces the dark pigment with white. Thus, an albino boa is largely yellowish white to white with yellow, peachy, orangish, or pinkish blotches. Neonates are more contrastingly colored than adults. A very light-colored albino boa that bears random splashes of dark pigment has been dubbed the "paradox" boa.

Blood boas: Hypomelanism reduces the amount of dark pigment present, allowing the normally muted oranges and reds to dominate. This is a variable characteristic and may

Albino Kenyan sand boas, **Eryx colubrinus loveridgei,** *are now readily available in the pet trade. (See page 37 for description.)*

produce a boa that has a ground color varying from reddish tan, through a peachy salmon, to a very rich red. The saddles and tail are darker red than the body. A particularly intense variation of this is called the "blood" boa. In this morph the red coloration is very dark reddish orange with darker reddish black banding.

Anerythric boas: Anerythric boas are very dark, silvery gray with black markings. Combinations of anerythrism crossed with hypomelanism are now being produced.

Striping

Striping instead of saddles has always interested boa enthusiasts. Striping, it seems, may be either the nongenetic result of incorrect incubation temperatures, or genetically replicable. Seldom is striping entire but, rather, is interspersed with an occasional normal-appearing dark saddle. When striping is present it is often best defined posteriorly.

Perhaps the most remarkable incidence of striping is present on the candycane morph boa constrictor. This boa is peppered black vertebrally. Below this on each side is a broad peach-colored stripe that is bordered ventrally with another stripe of peppered black. The sides are gray and more peppered black is present ventrolaterally. The tail striping is not noticeably more brilliant than the body.

The motley trait consists of light rounded dorsal blotches separated by very wide, dark crossbands.

The term *Arabesque* has been given to a strange-appearing morph having a peppering of dark pigment on the head and sides, narrow, light-centered dark crossbands, and somewhat enlarged light dorsal spots. The tail of this morph is usually dark rather than red.

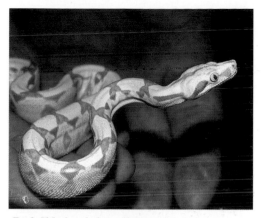

Rich Ihle bred this albino salmon boa.

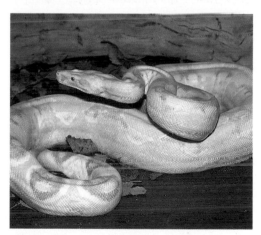

When albino common boa constrictors, Boa constrictor imperator, first became available they commanded prices of many thousands of dollars each.

As selective breeding programs increase in number, it seems inevitable that additional replicable patterns and morphs will appear in many boas and pythons. It will be interesting to see how popular they will be.

RAT SNAKES, KINGSNAKES, PINESNAKES, BULLSNAKES, AND GOPHER SNAKES

With several related genera, the rat snakes, kingsnakes, and gopher snakes are members of the subfamily Lampropeltinae. The majority of the lampropeltines are small enough—4 to 7 feet (1.2–2.1 m) long—when adult to be easily housed, have proven very hardy, and are easily bred. All are powerful constrictors, and the vast majority readily accept laboratory mice as their prey items.

Types of Rat Snakes

Collectively, the rat snakes, kingsnakes, and gopher snakes have caught the fancy of hobbyists as few other reptiles have. Together they are captive-bred by the tens of thousands annually, and with each passing season additional morphs of many species become available. In all of these snakes, albinism is the most commonly encountered aberrant factor, with pattern anomalies being second. However, one species, the corn snake, is not only the most normally variable, but has also proven the most plastic in breeding programs.

This attractive morph of the black rat snake, Elaphe o. obsoleta, *has been dubbed the "licorice stick" phase.*

Although the reproductive cycling of specimens collected from the wild may be exacting, once the proper regimen of cues has been learned, these snakes will often breed year after year and, if healthy and of good body weight, may multiclutch in any given year. If you are working with captive-bred and -hatched examples, these have proven easier to cycle reproductively than wild-collected specimens. Better yet, once you have succeeded in getting eggs from any of these snakes, the eggs have proven easy to incubate, to have a high hatch rate, and the babies of most are very easily raised.

Generally speaking, the corn snake is the most prolific species, having from one to several dozen proportionately small eggs.

Apricot Pueblan milksnakes,
Lampropeltis triangulum campbelli,
have the white rings replaced by
apricot orange.

A few decades ago, any aberrancies from the norm were truly worthy of mention. When Patti and I found a hatchling albino (amelanistic) corn crossing a Florida roadway in the mid 1970s, it was a cause for herpetocultural rejoicing. Today there are so many variations in color and pattern that all but the most spectacular—and albinos are not usually now considered all that spectacular—often go unsung.

Hatchling corn snakes are rather small. If healthy, a female corn snake will often have two clutches (more rarely, three) annually. The second clutch is often smaller than the first, and the third smaller yet.

Note: Multi-clutching is also known among other snake species.

The hatching ratio of the second and third clutches may be somewhat diminished.

Other species of American, Asian, and Eurasian rat snakes tend to have smaller clutches of proportionately larger eggs.

The closely allied milksnakes and kingsnakes have fairly small clutches—6 to 18 in number—of rather large eggs. The gopher, pine-, and bullsnakes have few but very large eggs. The hatchlings of some of these latter species may be large enough to overpower and consume a small adult lab mouse, which makes them easy to keep from the start.

Let's take a look at some of these coveted snakes.

History

As a group (and it is a *large* group), rat snakes occur naturally in North America, Central America, Asia, Malaysia, Indonesia, and Europe. Rat snakes are constricting snakes that became popular with hobbyists and breeders long before designer colors became routinely available. As currently defined taxonomically, the majority of both Old and New World species are included in the genus *Elaphe*. However, the Trans-Pecos and the Baja rat snakes are now in the genus *Bogertophis,* and the green rat snake and its relatives are *Senticolis*.

In those early predesigner color days of herpetoculture, collectors strove to acquire the brightest of the "normal" morphs of the red rat snake, also called the corn snake. Among these were the spectacular red on red-orange snake known as the Okeetee corn snake, the popular deep red on silver gray morph known as the Miami corn snake, despite the fact that the color is not restricted to South Florida, and the bright orange, red-tongued, Everglades rat snake. The various striped-tailed (or beauty) rat snakes of Asia, were also popular, again, the brighter the better.

Size

The corn snake, and its more westerly relative, the Great Plains rat snake, are moderately sized rat snakes. They top out at about 6 feet (1.8 m) in length, but are usually a foot or two (30–60 cm) smaller, and some adults may be little longer than 3 feet (91 cm). Corn snakes will eat frogs and lizards, but often attain their largest sizes when and where rodents are plentiful. On tiny keys and in the environs of big Florida cities, where lizards and frogs are more common than rodents, adult corn snakes are smaller than those from more rural areas.

Patterns and Colors

Today, when one visits any of several large herp expos one can see a dazzling array of patterns and colors in corn snakes. Most of the names relate to food, with names like sunglow, candycane, snow, butter, lavender, caramel, motley (named for the mottled pattern), black albino (which are really anerythristic corns that are more of a gray-brown than black), blizzard, and ghost. Some of the foremost breeders exhibiting at expos will set up a large display terrarium containing 10 or more morphs. Despite how common corn snakes have become, the display is always a crowd-stopper.

Why has the corn snake lent itself so well to the project of designing non-natural colors and patterns?

It seems likely that it is the snake's very own variability—its plasticity, if you will—that has so endeared it to hobbyists.

Although corn snakes are usually red on orange with a varying amount of black in the pattern, not only does the red of the saddles vary widely in intensity, but examples with gray, tan, or brown backgrounds, as well as an occasional albino, are well documented in nature. Hatchlings are often darker than adults, and full color potential may not be attained until the corn snake is several years old. With such natural variability, you'd expect interestingly colored and patterned offspring to spring forth from even random breedings. When selective breeding programs have been invoked, it seems that corn snake oddities now have almost become the norm.

Although albinism in wild populations is comparatively rare, a second phenomenon—anerythrism, the lack of red—is not. This is especially so in southwestern Florida where a large, and apparently viable, population of anerythristic wild corn snakes is present.

Adult albino radiated rat snakes, **Elaphe radiata**, *are somewhat darker in coloration than this hatchling.*

Anerythristic corn snakes are often found in southwestern Florida.

Anerythristic corn snakes are often erroneously referred to as "melanistics."

At first the goal was to merely develop and stabilize an albino (amelanistic) lineage. Dr. Bern Bechtel succeeded in this quest in the early 1960s. Since corn snakes are not only easily bred but are prolific as well, establishing albinism in background strains as diverse as Okeetee and Miami corn snakes was not at all difficult.

The various colors of the creamsicle corn snake, such as this albino, were derived from selectively crossing a Great Plains rat snake with a corn snake.

Snow corn: Then hobbyists combined amelanism—lack of black—with anerythrism—lack of red—and produced the snow corn, an interesting pale corn snake with yellowish or greenish blotches. If the blotches are vaguely pinkish, the snake is referred to as the "bubblegum" morph.

Creamsicle corn: Hobbyists then began to intergrade the Great Plains rat snake, a darker subspecies of the corn snake, with the corn snake. An amelanistic corn snake, bred to a normal Great Plains rat snake, yields heterozygous babies. When those babies are bred to each other, the magnificent creamsicle corn snake was the result. Other intergraded color morphs are on the way.

Black examples: Actual melanism has not yet been documented in either the corn or the Great Plains rat snakes, meaning no truly black examples have been found, but occasional very dark examples have been documented. To date, the darkest specimen seems to be an example of the Great Plains rat snake that was found in Kansas a few years ago. The snake is milk chocolate brown with deeper brown blotches. Dubbed a "chocolate" morph, the recessive genetics of this busily patterned, melanin-suffused snake are now being worked into breeding programs.

Lavender corn: It has been only within the last few years that the term lavender has come into play with corn snake genetics, but now it seems to be cropping up frequently in various settings. Rich Zuchowski of Serpenco was the developer of the lavender phase that resulted from breeding a snow corn to a corn snake that appeared to be of normal coloration. We must wonder what recessive genes this "normal" corn harbored. Pale brownish when

hatched, lavender corns develop a pale purplish pink sheen as they mature. Some examples have dark ruby-red eyes. The pale tan-gray body has darker gray saddles that do not have darker borders.

Blood-red corn: At one time, herpetoculturists felt that color morphs were inferior, that they possessed inherent weaknesses. This concern has been unfounded, with the exception of the blood-red corn. This particular color morph has proven to be a problematic morph. Hatchlings have large, deep red blotches separated by narrow gray bands (the bands are often pale orange dorsally) with a gray head that often lacks the spearpoint marking so characteristic of corn snakes. Blood corns also lack dark ventral checkerboarding. As the snakes mature they become even redder, with old adults—"old" being five years for a blood-red corn—almost unicolored blood red both above and below.

For some inexplicable reason, female bloodreds have large clutches of eggs. The hatchlings have often proven reluctant feeders, and are considered far more delicate than their counterparts of other colors.

Patterns

Corn snakes and Great Plains rat snakes are typically patterned with dark-outlined dorsal saddles that are darker than the ground color, as well as rows of discernible lateral spots. Hobbyists have now developed a "milksnake" phase that swings the dorsal blotches down into bands that reduce or incorporate the lateral spots.

Herpetoculturists have also changed the pattern of corn snake dorsal blotching to varying

patterns of dorsal striping. In many cases a light middorsal area is separated from the light sides by thin dark stripes. Often unbroken anteriorly, the dark stripes may either continue unbroken or break into dashes posteriorly. In another variant, dubbed the zigzag pattern, a dark-edged, broad, irregular, middorsal striping, often broken and interspersed with spots, is present. A third variant, the Aztec phase corn snake, has a very busy pattern of irregularly edged stripes, bars, and spots. This interesting phase is still of limited availability.

Another variant is the ruby-freckled corn snake, also known by the unflattering name of bloody rash corn snake. This is a white morph with a haphazard speckling of ruby red spots.

Herpetoculturists have long known that various color morphs, such as anerythrism and amelanism, are controlled by different genes. To account for this, the terms "type A" and "type B" are often heard. The offspring of an albino snake of type A when bred with an albino snake of type B will all be of normal (nonalbino) coloration, but all will be heterozygous (recessive) for both genetic packages.

Hypomelanism

Hypomelanism is a term that you will hear often when hobbyists are describing their corn and other rat snakes. The prefix "hypo" means reduced, not absent, just reduced, as opposed to "hyper," which means additional or accentuated. Although any snake having less black than its populational conspecifics may be termed hypomelanistic, the term is usually reserved by breeders to describe a distinct but variable hereditary reduction of melanin (black pigment). Hypomelanism may be selectively bred into virtually any color morph, including those having additional recessive alleles. It was by so doing that the ghost corn snake, a morph displaying both hypomelanism and type A anerythrism, was produced. The ghost corn has a pale gray backgound with darker-edged, medium gray-lavender saddles.

The ghost corn snake is one of several morphs to lack red.

"Hidden" Genetics

Butter yellow corn snakes, pewter corn snakes, lavender corn snakes, ghost corn snakes, blizzard corn snakes, blood-red corn snakes, piebald corn snakes—these and many additional morphs are currently available. The true colors and potential of many oddball corn snake colors may not be truly observable at hatching. In fact, without being carefully recorded, the genetics of the captive-born corn snake can become so thoroughly muddled that trying to determine the outcome of a given breeding can truly be an exercise in futility. Because of this, many corn snakes sold to pet stores by breeders may harbor any of several recessive genes. Should you happen to acquire and breed two captive-bred corn snakes, even if both are of normal coloration, it is possible, but not necessarily probable, to wind up with progeny of unexpected color phases.

Black Rat Snakes

The black rat snake is represented in the eastern United States by five subspecies and several well-established intergrades and color morphs. The Trans-Pecos rat snake of Texas, New Mexico, and adjacent Mexico, has two subspecies, but only one is currently in the hobby.

The subspecies of the black rat snake are the black, the yellow, the Everglades, the gray, and the Texas. The black rat has well-established, naturally occurring intergrades. These are the greenish rat snake and the Gulf Hammock variant. The black rat also has a natural color morph found in the northern Florida Keys, the Keys or Deckert's rat snake. Not all of these forms are popular in herpetoculture.

Because of the natural pattern diversity of the subspecies of the black rat snake, the species is of interest. The black, gray, and Texas subspecies are naturally strongly blotched both as hatchlings and adults, and they usually show little evidence of a lineate pattern. On the other hand, although the yellow and the Everglades rat snakes are strongly blotched at hatching, with growth the blotches diminish in contrast and prominent striping becomes evident. Typically a foot or so (30 cm) longer when adult than the corn snake, the black rat snake is a powerful snake of relatively heavy girth. The subspecies have been bred to produce stripeless, blotchless, licorice, high orange albinos and leucistic morphs.

The black rat snake, largely ignored by hobbyists when of its normal color, becomes interesting to many when aberrant. Two types of albinism—brindle and licorice stick morphs—have been developed.

Albino morphs of the black rat snake may be either t-positive or t-negative. If these two differing strains of albinism are bred together, the resulting F1 progeny will all be normally colored, a startling revelation to many novice breeders. The brindle morph is lighter in overall coloration than the normal black rat snake. It tends to have a variably grayish ground color and to have russet or mahogany overtones to the irregularly edged dark markings. The licorice stick morph has light (cream to light gray) sides and a black back. Hypomelanism has been noted occasionally in this subspecies. Hypomelanistic black rat snakes have pearl gray saddles on a light gray ground.

Albino bubblegum black rat snakes, not to be confused with bubblegum corn snakes, are occasionally available. These may involve the genes of either two (black and yellow) or three (black, yellow, and Everglades) subspecies of this rat snake. Bubblegum rat snakes have a

Interesting, but certainly not gaudy, the caramel corn snake is one of the newer color phases.

white ground color over which plays a variable amount of yellow to orange coloration.

Gray rat snake: Although albinos of the gray rat snake have been found, this contrastingly blotched race has never become popular with herpetoculturists. However, albino yellow rat snakes seem to sell well but are not very colorful. Against the white body color is a series of yellowish dorsal blotches, but the four dark lines, a hallmark of normally colored yellow rat snakes, are often only vaguely discernible. Two unusual color morphs were found in Alva, Florida, about a decade ago. One, the darker of the two, looked much like a brindle phase black rat snake but had the four stripes characteristic of a yellow rat snake. The second, thought to be axanthic, had a ground color of tannish brown, four well-developed dark stripes, and orange eyes.

Everglades rat snake: Of the races of the black rat snake, the Everglades rat snake is

traditionally the most richly colored. Once common in Florida's Everglades, from which its common name was taken, this pale-striped, red-tongued, orange-bodied, largely arboreal snake has long been one of the more popular rat snakes. Today, because of the draining of that vast marsh, the less colorful yellow rat snake has all but outcompeted and replaced the Everglades rat snake. Wild examples of the latter are now truly uncommon; however, captive-breeding programs, selectively matching the most colorful and typical examples of the Everglades rat snake with each other, have again reproduced the race, and in some instances even enhanced the diagnostic characters of the subspecies. Hypomelanism has now occurred in this race. Hypomelanistic adults of this morph can be unbelievably brilliant orange with stripes that are all but invisible.

Other Morphs

Selective breeding programs have also stabilized the burnt-orange, striped and blotched rat snake from the northern Florida Keys. Although biologically nothing more than a

Hypomelanism has enhanced the beauty of the Everglades rat snake, **Elaphe obsoleta rossalleni.**

yellow rat snake, the beautiful color and pattern of this population has caught and held the interest of hobbyists.

Texas rat snake: Normally colored Texas rat snakes are neither particularly pretty nor possessed of a benign disposition. In fact, the defensive strikes of adults encountered in the wild can be positively intimidating. It is small wonder then that, until aberrant colorations became available, Texas rat snakes were not popular.

However, today, Texas rat snakes are available in a spectacularly beautiful, dark-eyed, alabaster-white, leucistic morph, as well as a pink-eyed albino, and a white-sided pattern anomaly, quite similar in appearance to the licorice stick morph of the black rat snake. Probably because of the extensive inbreeding the comparatively small gene pool of leucistic specimens has undergone, many examples of this phase now have bugged or "pop eyes."

Decried by most hobbyists, a few herpetoculturists have embraced this anomaly and are perpetuating the characteristic. Another morph is an eerie-appearing form that lacks dorsal, lateral, and most head scales. Because of the lack of supporting labial and chin scales, the scaleless morph often has a curiously underslung lower jaw.

Trans-Pecos rat snake: The Trans-Pecos rat snake is a slender, supple, beautifully colored, gentle-dispositioned serpent of the Chihuahuan Desert. In its normally colored morph, this snake is typified by a series of large, dark Hs along its back. In extreme southwestern Texas an unusual blonde form occurs. On this, rather than Hs, the dorsal markings are rounded blotches, often with light centers. A very few albino specimens have been found, but these are not yet generally available. Rather recently, a pretty steel gray morph has been developed and is now becoming increasingly popular.

Asian and Eurasian Rat Snakes

It is only within the last 10 to 15 years that Asian and Eurasian rat snakes have become popular with hobbyists. Of the more than 30 Old World species, only a handful have been recorded as having aberrant color forms. Albinistic and axanthic copperhead rat snakes, *E. moellendorffi*, have been documented but are not yet available in herpetoculture. A naturally occurring population of albino Japanese rat snakes, *E. climacophora*, has long been known, but is rigidly protected by Japan, therefore rarely available in herpetoculture. Asymmetrical eye development, probably the result of decades of inbreeding, is not uncommon in these snakes.

Cheryl Bott has acquired a beautiful pair of albino striped-tailed rat snakes, *E. taeniura taeniura*, and is hoping to be able to offer babies to hobbyists within the next few years. Blotched anteriorly, the pattern becomes linear posteriorly, thus the common name.

The most commonly seen albino Asian rat snake in American herpetoculture is the pretty, but usually feisty, radiated rat snake, *E. radiata*. In actions and reactions this snake is more like a fast-moving, bad-tempered racer than a rat snake. It is a striped snake with an interesting head pattern and derives the common name from the several dark lines radiating outward from the eyes.

Since some hobbyists are reluctant to advertise their aberrant specimens until they have actually established a viable breeding program, there are undoubtedly species besides those we have mentioned now in captivity. New and interesting patterns and pattern-color combinations of these as well as of the well-established

Pretty even when normally colored, blonde and silver morphs of the Trans-Pecos rat snake, **Bogertophis subocularis,** *are coveted by hobbyists.*

old favorites will continue to appear in herpeto-culture. Is there a chance for you, as a new hob-byist, to develop something new?

The answer is unequivocally yes! Get involved.

Types of Kingsnakes and Milksnakes

The kingsnakes and milksnakes (genus *Lampropeltis*) are closely allied to the rat snakes (genus *Elaphe*).

Like the rat snakes, kingsnakes and milk-snakes are hardy, easily kept, and easily bred, and their eggs easily incubated. They lend themselves well to intraspecific intergradation as well as to intergeneric and interspecific hybridization. Because of this, kingsnake/gopher snake hybrids or kingsnake/rat snake hybrids are often available to hobbyists.

The members of the eastern kingsnake group are adult at from 3 to 5.5 feet (91–165 cm) in length, while those of the milksnake group are from 2 to 6 feet (61–183 cm) in length. Of the kingsnakes and milksnakes the California kingsnake, *L. getula californiae,* and the Honduran milksnake, *L. triangulum*

hondurensis, are available in the greatest diver-sity of colors. This seems understandable since both of these occur naturally in several color and pattern morphs.

The California kingsnake is the westernmost representative of the many subspecies of the eastern kingsnake. Typically, the California kingsnake has a brown to black ground color and is patterned with either bands or a stripe (rarely both) of cream to white. Although not colorful, this is a pretty snake. Albinos of both the striped and the banded morphs are rela-tively common in nature, so it was no wonder that early in the dawn of designer snakes, sev-eral strains of albino California kingsnakes were developed and stabilized.

Then other colors and patterns became available.

Colors and Patterns

Lavender Cal-kings, albinos with a purplish cast, were produced, as were normally colored Cal-kings with very abnormal patterns. Such names as banana, in which the light scales are a creamy yellow, half-white, also referred to as 50-50, high yellow, a primarily yellow Cal-king, and ruby-eyed albinos came to be associated with California kingsnakes, and virtually all were available in both the banded and the striped morphs.

Albinism has also occurred, but not as fre-quently, in speckled kingsnakes, *L. g. holbrooki,* in Peninsula kingsnake intergrades, *L. g. getula* x *L. g. floridana* (erroneously referred to as

This pale (hypomelanistic?) California kingsnake, **Lampropeltis getula californiae,** *was dubbed the "banana-fudge phase" by The Gourmet Rodent.*

Many color phases of the speckled kingsnake, **Lampropeltis getula holbrooki,** *are now available.*

L. g. floridana by hobbyists), and in the Florida kingsnakes from the southernmost tip of the Florida peninsula. These are the true *L. g. floridana,* but are still referred to by the out-dated but well-established names of South Florida kingsnake, *L. g. brooksi,* by hobbyists.

Hypomelanism has now occurred in this latter race of kingsnakes. The hatchlings are a spectac-ular fire-orange that fades with growth and advancing age to a remarkably pretty yellow.

At least one albino desert kingsnake, *L. g. splendida,* has been found. Strangely, it has been years since the albinos of this race were offered in the pet trade.

Although albinism does not seem to be nat-urally known in either the eastern or western black kingsnakes, *L. g. nigra* or *L. g. nigrita,* or in the eastern kingsnake, *L. g. getula,* hobbyists have intergraded these races with albinos of other forms, then selectively bred back for the desired patterns.

Apalachicola lowlands kingsnake: Neither does naturally occurring albinism seem to be known in the interesting population of kingsnakes that occur in the lowlands of the Apalachicola River on Florida's panhandle. Currently considered an unusual and diverse-appearing intergrade of the Florida and eastern kingsnakes, these snakes were originally described as *L. g. goini,* and were given the com-mon name of Goin's or blotched kings. Despite the fact that these names are no longer valid, hobbyists continue to use them. The snakes in this population occur naturally in patternless,

striped, and wide-blotched morphs. Although they have proven difficult to find in the wild, enough have been collected to firmly establish all morphs in captive-breeding programs. Hob-byists seem to favor the striped and patternless phases over the blotched form. Like many of the eastern races of the kingsnake, hatchlings of the Apalachicola lowlands kingsnakes often have a suffusion of orange or pink on their sides. Normally, this fades with growth and by the time the snake has gone through a couple of sheds, the suffusion of brilliance has all but disappeared. However, Sheila Rodgers of Gulf Coast Reptiles began selectively breeding the most brightly colored of her hatchlings, and has now succeeded in producing kingsnakes on which the orange suffusion is not only perma-nent, fading only somewhat with age and growth, but is present over virtually the entire snake. This is probably a form of hypomelanism. The end result is a spectacularly pretty snake.

Prairie kingsnake: In addition to the eastern kingsnake group, albinism is also known in the prairie kingsnake, *L. calligaster calligaster,* a common species of the mid-United States.

Although typically a dark-blotched grayish snake, some examples are striped, and albinos of both morphs are known. As babies, these albinos are strawberry on white snakes, but the adults tend to be more orange and yellow.

Other Species

Besides the typical kingsnakes, there are several species that typically bear blotches, bands, or rings of red, yellow (or white), and black (or gray). Among these are the gray-banded kingsnake (*L. alterna*), the San Luis Potosi kingsnake (*L. mexicana*), the Ruthven's kingsnake (*L. ruthveni*), and the many races of the milksnake (*L. triangulum*). Captive-breeding programs for virtually all of these have long been in place.

Albinism has cropped up in the gray-banded kingsnake (rarely), but does not yet seem to have been stabilized in that species. It is better represented and firmly established in the Ruthven's kingsnake and in several subspecies of the milksnake.

Gray-banded kingsnake: The gray-banded kingsnake is a canyonland snake of the Chihuahuan Desert. It naturally occurs in a wide range of colors and patterns. At one extreme

Although beauty is in the eye of the beholder, most who see it think of the albino Ruthven's kingsnake, Lampropeltis ruthveni, as a beautiful snake.

is a very narrow-banded, primarily gray and black, "alterna" phase, and at the opposite extreme is the very brilliantly colored red, black, gray, and white "blairi" phase. Between these two extremes are any number of intermediate phases. This snake boasts a large contingent of very enthusiastic devotees who seek representative examples from every specific canyon and rock in which the snake has been found. As might be expected, there are a great many captive-breeding programs that selectively breed for particular characteristics. Occasional "sports," such as striped examples, appear in these programs, but none have yet been stabilized in numbers sufficient to assure their continued appearance in herpetoculture.

Ruthven's kingsnake: The Ruthven's kingsnake is also called the Queretaro kingsnake. Most of the specimens now in captivity seem to have originated from the Mexican state of the same name. The species is also known from the Mexican state of Michoacan. If normally colored, Ruthven's kingsnake is brightly ringed in red, black, and yellow or white and has a black nose with some gray on the snout. The bands are usually rather evenly edged dorsally and laterally but are irregular ventrally. Albinos of this snake seem to have first made their appearance in herpetoculture in the mid 1980s. At that time the asking price was so high that only the most dedicated of breeders could consider purchasing this interesting morph. Today the price has dropped considerably, but still remains in the hundreds of dollars.

Albinos of Milksnakes

Albinos of several of the milksnakes are well known, and selective breeding has assured that many will remain available for generations to come. Additionally, some pattern abnormalities are selectively bred for.

✔ One of the newest and most interesting of the latter is the bullet morph of the Mexican milksnake, *L. t. annulata*. Normally a prettily ringed red, black, and yellow snake, in the bullet phase the rings are reduced to yellow-centered black circles along the back.

✔ Albino eastern milksnakes, *L. t. triangulum*, have been found occasionally, but do not seem to have gained entry in the pet marketplace.

✔ The same holds true for scarlet kingsnakes, *L. t. elapsoides*. Both albinos and an interesting "pastel" phase have been found, but neither are yet represented in herpetoculture. This might well be due to the tiny size of the neonate scarlet kings. They are so small that they are able to eat only baby lizards or tiny pieces of pinky mice. This factor makes the race difficult for many hobbyists to maintain.

✔ Albinos of both the Sinaloan milksnake, *L. t. sinaloae*, and Nelson's milksnake, *L. t. nelsoni*, are well represented in the hobby. Both of these races occur in northwestern mainland Mexico. The Sinaloan milksnake is noted for its very broad red rings. The pattern of the Nelson's milksnake is somewhat busier. These are both hardy snakes and both normal and albinos are often available from specialty breeders or straight from their breeders.

✔ Pueblan milksnakes, *L. t. campbelli*, are currently being selectively bred for two color factors: a pretty apricot ground color and a "sockhead," a posterior extension of the black nose and head well back onto the neck. This makes the snake look as if its nose, head, and neck has been dipped in black paint.

Honduran Milksnakes

Of all of the milksnakes, the Honduran, *L. t. hondurensis*, is by far the most diverse both in color and pattern. This is a pretty, large—to about 5 feet (152 cm) in length—milksnake that naturally occurs in at least three color forms. These are a bicolor (primarily red and black rings with a very little yellow occasionally showing), a tricolor (prominent red, black, and yellow rings), and a tangerine (deep orange, paler orange, and black rings) phase. From these, chance and selective breeding have developed another half dozen or more morphs.

Selective breeding programs have even enhanced the naturally occurring tangerine coloration. Independently, Norm Damm and Bill and Kathy Love began breeding for brilliance into their tangerine Hondurans. Norm dubbed his brilliant orange-on-orange creation the "Damn strain," and Bill called their glowing beauty the "tangerine dream."

With the enhanced tangerines and other phases available, it is small wonder that other color morphs began to spontaneously appear. Two of the first among these were the albino and the anerythristic phases. With white replacing the black rings, the albino Honduran milksnake was a beautiful white, bright red, and butter yellow snake. It immediately found favor with herpetoculturists. Unlike anerythristic corn snakes, which are virtually devoid of red pigment, the red of the anerythristic Honduran milksnake is present but is muted and dull and the yellow bands are white. Only the black is sharp and crisp.

Many additional color and pattern morphs of the Honduran milksnake are also available.

Among these are a striped tangerine, a striped tricolor, hypomelanistic, pinstriped, disappearing pattern, snow, and ghost Hondurans. The striped tangerine morph is a beautiful but irregularly marked morph. The body is intense orange and the broken lineate markings are ebony. It will likely take several additional generations of selective breeding before the striping comes even close to being perfected.

Types of Pinesnakes

Pine, bull, and gopher snakes are all members of the genus *Pituophis,* and they bear many similarities. As a group, these snakes are referred to as the pinesnakes. They are good-sized—to 8 feet (2.4 m) in length—snakes of medium body weight, and all bear some version of dark splotches or stripes on a tan to yellow to white background. They characteristically have strongly keeled scales. They are persistent burrowers and powerful constrictors. The pinesnakes are native to North America, being found as far north as Canada and as far south as Guatemala. A few

populations are found on islands off the coast of Baja California. These are snakes of sandy soils. Those in the East occur in forested areas; those in the West are found in pasturelands, rocky aridlands, and open woodlands.

Members of this group eat rodents and other small mammals. The gopher and bullsnakes add in birds and birds' eggs; young gopher snakes also eat large insects. Pinesnakes prefer pocket gophers. Rodents are followed into their burrows, and are killed there by being pressed against the sides of the tunnel until they suffocate.

Unlike most other snakes, the pinesnakes can be found quite far from water. The females are egg-layers, laying, as a rule, fewer, larger eggs rather than quantities of smaller eggs. The young are proportionately large when hatched.

All of these snakes have a modified glottis. When they exhale strongly, the moving air is emitted in a loud and characteristic hiss.

Although many of the pinesnake group would rather hiss than fight, these snakes do not hesitate to strike and bite if provoked, and they can bite *hard.* And purely as a natural his-

Designer colors in the Honduran milksnake, Lampropeltis triangulum hondurensis, *now vary from a pure white snow phase (left) to an enhanced tangerine (right).*

The Florida pinesnake, **Pituophis melanoleucus mugitus,** *is now readily available in an albino morph.*

tory note, I'll point out that the larger a snake is, the bigger its mouth.

Listed on the following page are the most commonly available pinesnakes and their morphs. Not all of the pinesnakes are listed here; some of them are rare, protected, or otherwise unknown in captivity. Not all are available in any color morphs.

Let's look at each group within the pinesnakes.

The pine snakes, all subspecies of *Pituophis melanoleucus,* grow to about 66 inches (168 cm). They are all essentially dark-blotched snakes with a pallid background. There are four subspecies.

Northern pinesnake: The Northern pine, *Pituophis melanoleucus melanoleucus,* is found in southern New Jersey, Kentucky, the Carolinas, Georgia, and part of northern Alabama. This is a white or pallid snake with very dark blotches along its back. Northern pines have heavily keeled scales with two small pits, called apical pits, near the tip of each scale. These snakes are active during the day, although as summer heats up they tend to become active later and later in the day. They spend most of their time in burrows, but they can climb more or less adeptly. They eat small mammals, including squirrels, gophers, rats, and rabbits, and birds and birds' eggs. Morphs include an albino and a white form.

Black pinesnake: The black pinesnake, *P. m. lodingi,* comes from an extremely limited range that includes southwestern Alabama, southeastern Mississippi, and Washington Parish in Louisiana. It has intergraded with the Florida

pinesnake on the far western tip of Florida's panhandle. Black pinesnakes are usually 36 to 60 inches long (91–152 cm); the record was 89 inches (225 cm). In the wild, the black pinesnake spends its days (and nights) underground, exploring stumpholes, armadillo burrows, gopher tortoise burrows, or the tunnels it digs itself. It eats mice, birds and their eggs, other reptile eggs, and rabbits, but its favorite food is the pocket gopher.

Although its limited range and fossorial habits mean this snake is rarely observed in the wild, it is a staple in the pet industry. Its willingness to live in confined areas (a cage is just a modified burrow, if there's enough cover), to eat quantities of mice, to breed in captivity (four to eight eggs per clutch), and its attractive coloration are all factors that matter to breeders, hobbyists, and pet stores. No color morphs are yet available; this snake is just bred to produce the blackest black possible.

Louisiana pinesnake: The Louisiana pinesnake, *P. ruthveni,* is another subterranean pinesnake. It prefers the longleaf pine areas of western Louisiana and east Texas, but as those forests have been logged, the range of their favorite prey (a pocket gopher) has decreased.

Commonly Available Pinesnakes

	Albino	Other Colors and Patterns
Northern pinesnake (Pituophis m. melanoleucus)	yes	white, high red
Black pinesnake (P. m. lodingi)	–	all black is most desired
Florida pinesnake (P. m. mugitus)	yes	snow
Louisiana pinesnake (P. ruthveni)	–	–
Bullsnake (P. catenifer sayi)	yes	amelanistic, anerythristic, axanthic, and pattern anomalies
Pacific gopher snake (P. c. catenifer)	yes	striped albino, Applegate phase, striped albino
Sonoran gopher (P. c. affinis)	yes	–
San Diegan gopher (P. c. pumilis)	yes	–

The range of the Louisiana pinesnake has also decreased. Now it is considered a rare reptile and is on the endangered list for Texas. Its current range is a few disjunct old-timber areas in west Texas and in eastern Louisiana. In size, the Louisiana pinesnake ranges from 36 to 60 inches (91–152 cm); the record is just under 6 feet (183 cm). Because of its rarity, very little breeding has been done with this snake and no color morphs have been described.

Florida pinesnake: The Florida pine (P. m. mugitus) is found in Florida, except for the southern tip, through southeastern Georgia, and southernmost South Carolina. It is rare in Florida and protected in that state and in Georgia. Interestingly enough, Florida recognizes that the albino morphs are a derived form, and those can be legally bought, sold, and traded. This snake prefers open pinelands and upland sandhill areas, although it spends the majority of its time in burrows. The home range of this snake—the area over which a snake regularly ranges—is sizeable. Males use up to 247 acres, second only to the indigo snake.

Both snow and albino morphs have been developed in this snake.

Types of Bullsnakes

The bullsnake, P. catenifer sayi, is the largest of the pinesnakes, frequently reaching a length of 80 inches (203 cm); the record is 100 inches (254 cm). It is found from Alberta and Saskatchewan to the tip of Texas, from Central New Mexico and Colorado and the Rocky Mountains front range, eastward to Minnesota, Wisconsin, Illinois, and the eastern half of Texas. Bullsnakes are yellow to tan, with dark blotches along the back, and each blotch outlined in a darker tone of the same shade. A stripe runs from the corner of the eye to the back edge of the mouth.

Bullsnakes like mostly dry, open-country terrain from sea level to about 7,000 feet (2,134 m). They feed on burrowing rodents,

ground-nesting birds, and an occasional snake. Juveniles eat lizards and insects. Like the pinesnake, the bullsnake is active during the day, but hot weather may move its activity pattern to early morning or the evening hours. Most of its activity is limited to hunting through rodent burrows, seeking birds or their nests, or resting. Color morphs of the bullsnake include white-sided, albino, anerythristic, amelanistic, and axanthic, in addition to pattern anomalies.

Types of Gopher Snakes

The gopher snakes are all subspecies of *P. catenifer*, and are divded up into ten (more or less) subspecies. Color or pattern morphs have been found in only four subspecies. The gopher snakes range in length from 4 to 6 feet (122–183 cm) and may reach 7 feet (210 cm). The exception is the much smaller Santa Cruz gopher snake, found off the northwestern cost of Baja California; it averages about 3 feet (91 cm).

Sonoran gopher snakes: Sonoran gopher snakes, *P. c. affinis*, are cream to yellow snakes with multiple brown or dark brown dorsal and lateral blotches. Typically, a dark line runs from beneath one eye, across the eye and the top of the head, down below the other eye. The range is the western states, from Canada southward to Baja California and Mexico. In Texas, the Sonoran intergrades with the bullsnake. The diet consists of rodents and small birds. An albino morph is available.

San Diegan gopher snake: The San Diegan gopher (*P. s. annectans*) is found in a narrow swath from extreme southern California to mid-Baja California. An albino morph has been developed.

Pacific gopher snake: The Pacific gopher snake, *P. c. catenifer*, is from the northwestern coast of California. This is a naturally variable snake, being found in the wild in both blotched and striped forms. Albino blotched and striped morphs are available. The Applegate phase is a lavender albino.

The Pacific gopher snake is also available in a spectacular lavender phase.

Albinism has been documented in snakes as diverse as the tricolored scarlet snakes, Cemophora coccinea *ssp., and black racers,* Coluber constrictor *ssp.*

Varieties

✔ Scarlet snakes are small—20 to 30 inches (51–76 cm)—kingsnake relatives of the south-eastern and southcentral United States. In one or another of its subspecies the racer, a 3- to 5-foot-long (91–152 cm) species, ranges from coast to coast. Pattern abnormalities, where the normal banding has been reduced to yellow-centered black dorsal spots or even a yellow-centered black linear pattern, have also been noted in scarlet snakes.

✔ Anerythristic and albino mud snakes, *Farancia abacura* ssp., have been found. The mud snake is a big—4 to 5 feet (122–152 cm)—shiny-scaled aquatic snake of the southeastern United States. It is typically black and red in coloration. Anerythristic individuals are black and white and the albino juvenile was pinkish white with strawberry red lateral wedges.

✔ Albinism changed the appearance of the tiny—10 to 15 inches (25–38 cm)—leaf-litter-dwelling pinewoods snake, *Rhadinea flavilata*,

This albino queen snake, Regina septemvittata, *was found in a North Carolina stream.*

of the southeastern United States from mahogany brown with a darker head to having a creamy white body with peach overtones and a reddish head.

Hog-nosed Snakes

Albinism is known in all three species of the hog-nosed snake, *Heterodon* sp., but this and erythrism have been perpetuated by hobbyists to the greatest extent in the western hog-nosed snake, *H. nasicus* ssp. This is because the western hog-nosed snake is more easily main-tained in captivity than the other two species.

To a species, the hog-noses are proportion-ately stout, world-class bluffers. Their common name is derived from the upturned rostral, most accentuated in the southern and western species, a feature that probably serves the snakes well as they root through the sand for their buried prey. The preferred prey of the eastern and the southern hog-nosed snakes is toads. Although an occasional captive can be tricked into accepting a small mouse, most eastern and southern hog-nosed snakes do not do well on a mouse diet. On the other hand, the various races of the western hog-nosed

snake have a far broader spectrum diet. Besides toads, these snakes will accept frogs, lizards, other snakes, nestlings of ground-nesting birds, and nestling rodents.

Hog-nosed snakes are known for their unusual defensive habits. Rather than striking and biting as many snakes would, when sufficiently threatened hog-nosed snakes flatten the anterior of their body into a cobralike hood, open their mouths widely, and thrash from side to side. If the threat then diminishes, the snake discontinues the display and goes its way. If the threat remains, the hog-nose begins a spasmodic writhing, first right side up, then rolls belly up, writhes some more, lolls the tongue out of the open mouth, and becomes still, to all appearances dead. That is, to all appearances save one: If you roll the "dead" snake right side up, it will turn itself upside down again, and remain so until it feels the coast is clear.

Hog-noses have greatly enlarged rear teeth and a somewhat toxic saliva. Not that the snakes of this genus are prone to biting, but the large teeth and toxic saliva suggest that it is best if you do not get bitten.

Whether in the red or the albino phase (both pictured), the dusty hog-nosed snake, Heterodon nasicus gloydi, is an easily kept and much coveted snake.

Females of all three species are considerably larger than the males.

Eastern hog-nose: Although it is usually smaller, the eastern hog-nosed snake, *H. platirhinos*, can occasionally attain 3.5 feet (107 cm) in length. In coloration this is a very variable species, having tan morphs, red morphs, black morphs, and olive morphs. An occasional albino has been found. Although hobbyists are enchanted by this snake, because they are specialized feeders few long-range breeding programs have been successful. This species ranges over much of the eastern United States.

Southern hog-nose: The smaller southern hog-nosed snake, *H. simus*, is adult at 24 inches (61 cm) in length but is usually at least 6 inches (15 cm) smaller. This is a species of the coastal plain from North Carolina to Louisiana and ranges southward to central Florida. Far less variable in coloration than its more northerly relative, it is clad in variable tans and browns. Occasional albinos have been found. No long-term breeding projects are in effect.

Western hog-nose: On the other hand, many hobbyists are breeding the various subspecies of the western hog-nosed snake. These top out at about 3 feet (91 cm) in length but are usually somewhat smaller. The Plains subspecies, *H. n. nasicus*, is quite standard in pattern, but variable in ground color. Normally having scales of tan, gray, and brown, it also occurs naturally in beautiful reds. A number of albinos have been found. A second subspecies, the Mexican hog-nosed snake, *H. n. kennerlyi*, is also a hobbyist favorite. Recently, Mike Price has found some examples with a chalk-white ground color and will be selectively breeding to perpetuate this characteristic.

House Snakes

The African brown house snake, *Lamprophis fuliginosus*, is a supple constrictor of moderate size—24 to 30 inches (61–76 cm). Females are the larger sex. This species of house snake varies from nearly black, through various browns, to a beautiful russet in coloration. Thin whitish or pinkish lines are often present on the side of the head. Hobbyists have long selectively bred in an effort to brighten the russet coloration. Piebald specimens are known but are rare and do not seem to have yet been incorporated into successful breeding programs; however, albino house snakes are now being bred by several hobbyists. Once fully acclimated, brown house snakes are easily bred and healthy females may produce three or four clutches annually. It will be interesting to see what new morphs spontaneously appear as breeding programs increase in number.

Garter, Ribbon, and Water Snakes

The garter, ribbon, and water snakes are members of the colubrine subfamily Natricinae. Most of the garter and ribbon snakes are adult at about 30 inches (76 cm) in length. Many of the water snakes can attain an adult length of 4 feet (122 cm) or longer. Most of the garter snakes eat worms, amphibians, and fish; some will also accept nestling rodents. The ribbon snakes prefer a diet of small fish and tadpoles, but will often accept a small frog or salamander. The water snakes eat fish and amphibians. The related queen snake, a member of the

Cheryl Bott is hoping to perpetuate albino brown house snakes, **Lamprophis fuliginosus.**

crayfish snake group, prefers soft-shelled cray-fish, but may opportunistically accept other aquatic organisms. Many of the species are common in the wild, and albinism is known in several species and subspecies. The natricines are greatly favored by European hobbyists, but are just now becoming popular with American herpetoculturists. As might be expected, breeding programs concentrate largely on albinos.

Eastern garter snake: Of the garter snakes, the eastern, *Thamnophis s. sirtalis*, is the most variable. It occurs naturally in striped and checkered patterns, and with ground colors of black, brown, tan, greenish, or orange. Many albino specimens have been found in the wild, and selective breeding programs perpetuating this trait are now in place. Neonate albinos are beautiful white snakes with pink highlights, but with advancing age and growth the ground color becomes a little creamier and the markings less contrasting.

In one or another of its many subspecies, the eastern garter snake is found from coast to coast and from Canada to northern Mexico. Although less variable in ground color, many of the more westerly subspecies have a fair amount of bright red on the sides. Albinos of at least one of these, the red-sided garter snake, *T. s. parietalis*, are known.

Flame garter snake: An exciting new morph was introduced to the hobby by Dr. Phil Blais. This is the spectacular "flame garter." Derived from reddish colored Canadian garter snakes, this morph has brilliant red upper sides and is quite probably the most colorful garter snake now available in herpetoculture.

Plains garter snake: Both albino and leucistic examples of the Plains garter snake, *T. radix*, have been found. The former are white and pinkish with red eyes, but the latter are a stark, unmarked white with black eyes. Of these two aberrancies only the albinos are being selectively perpetuated.

Checkered garter snake: The checkered garter snake, *T. m. marcianus*, is a beautiful checkmarked species with a black splotch on each side of the neck. They are an abundant species of the southcentral and southwestern United States and much of Mexico. In this arid habitat they are usually found along permanent and semipermanent watercourses. Certainly pretty enough to warrant notice even when of normal gray, black, and yellow color, albinos, which are rather regularly found in the wild, are an eyecatching pinkish red on white. Many hobbyists breed this species.

The flame garter snake, developed by Phil Blais, is a very red (erythristic) morph of the eastern garter snake, **Thamnophis s. sirtalis.**

Hypomelanism (paleness) has occurred in the brown water snake, **Nerodia taxispilota.**

Although they are not often kept by hobbyists, color aberrancies of several other thamnophine species are known.

✔ One or two albinos of the Peninsula ribbon snake, *Thamnophis sauritus sackenii*, have been found, as has a jet black melanistic specimen.

✔ Brown water snakes, *Nerodia taxispilota*, are huge, sullen-looking snakes that can be found along southeastern watercourses. They normally bear prominent light-edged dark brown blotches on a lighter ground color. Recently a few hypomelanistic specimens having a notably lighter color overall have been found near Lake Okeechobee, Florida.

✔ James McQueen and Shannon Branton have told us about a big albino diamondback water snake, *Nerodia r. rhombifer*, that used to live in a western Kentucky lake and could often be seen basking in the vicinity of a dock.

✔ Another albino of this chain-patterned dark brown on lighter brown snake was kept for years by Chris McQuade. It was never successfully bred.

✔ Albinos of both the northern water snake, *N. s. sipedon*, and the Florida water snake, *N. fasciata pictiventris*, are also known but are not yet being captive-bred.

✔ The queen snake, *Regina septemvittata*, is a stream, river, swamp-edge, and lake-dwelling water snake relative of the eastern and central United States. One or two albino specimens of this interesting but difficult-to-keep snake have been found.

VENOMOUS SNAKES

Although they are more difficult to handle and not always looked at closely by the homeowners on whose land they are found, venomous snakes have had their share of color, pattern, and scale aberrancies documented. Of these, albinism and melanism seem the most commonly encountered phenomena.

Types of Rattlesnakes

Both albino and hypomelanistic northwestern neotropical rattlesnakes and prairie rattlesnakes have been occasionally found. They are beautiful, commanding creatures that are possessed of short tempers and virulent venom. The prairie rattlesnake is an abundant species in the western central United States, as well as adjacent Mexico and Canada; the northwestern neotropical rattlesnake occurs in southwestern Mexico.

Because of the ground coloration of many examples, the prairie rattler is often referred to as the green rattlesnake. It is strongly blotched, and although it can be formidably defensive, it is an attractive serpent. Since it is the dark pigments that are variably deficient when albinism and hypolemelanism occur, the resulting whitish snakes are starkly beautiful, being clad in scales

Albino monacled cobras, Naja naja kaouthia, *have long been bred by hobbyists. This example, in a defensive pose, was photographed by Matt Lerer.*

bearing variable combinations of white, cream, and yellow.

Albino northwestern neotropical rattlesnakes are somewhat less different from the normal than are albinos of many other species. This is because these impressive 5-foot-long (152 cm) snakes are normally clad mostly in tans, having darker neck stripes and diamond outlines dorsally. With less melanin typically present, even when it is entirely absent the resulting ground

TIP

Warning!

Venomous snakes should be handled only by experienced hobbyists or professionals, and many states regulate who may keep these snakes. If you want to handle venomous snakes, apprentice yourself to an experienced handler and avoid potentially deadly situations.

color is a creamy tan and the darker markings are pinkish tan. Beautiful and instantly noticeable, but in this species, the term albino definitely does not equate to whiteness.

Diamondback rattlesnakes: Many aberrant colors and patterns of the eastern diamondback rattlesnake, a 4.5- to 6-foot-long (135–183 cm) species of the southeastern United States, have been documented. These include albino, leucistic, patternless, axanthic, hypomelanistic, and striped morphs. To date, eastern diamondbacks have proven difficult to breed in captivity, and many of these phases are known only from specimens taken from the wild.

On the other hand, the western diamondback rattlesnake, a similarly sized species of the Southern Plains and western states and northern Mexico, is being captive-bred in quite con-

Mike Price photographed this patternless western diamondback rattlesnake, Crotalus atrox, *from the collection of Tim Cole.*

siderable numbers and in several aberrant morphs. This impressive and often irascible snake occurs in albino, patternless, melanistic, erythristic, and scaleless morphs.

Albinism is also known to occur in timber rattlesnakes and Southern Pacific rattlesnakes.

The eastern massasauga is a small—24 to 36 inches long (61–91 cm)—marsh-swampland rattlesnake from the eastern central United States. It occurs naturally in both a dark-blotched brown phase and a variably black phase. This latter morph is eagerly sought by herpetoculturists and is now being captive-bred in some numbers.

The red phase of the somewhat smaller but closely related Carolina pygmy rattlesnake is also a coveted snake. This beautiful morph is restricted in natural distribution to eastern North Carolina, where it is protected by law. However, some specimens currently held in captivity are now being bred by hobbyists and the intent is to develop the reddest possible coloration.

Types of Vipers

Eyelash viper: The eyelash viper is an arboreal fer-de-lance relative that ranges southward from southern Mexico to Ecuador. This is one of the most naturally polymorphic (variably colored) snake species known, and despite its venomous properties it is popular with herpetoculturists. Eyelash vipers are being linebred for specific color and pattern traits. Hobbyists are particularly fond of the yellow (or yellow and pink) orapel morph. A yellow morph having broad moss green bands is also a favorite, as is a busily patterned moss green and strawberry morph now dubbed the "Christmas phase."

Copperheads

The copperhead is a beautiful russet on tan-colored venomous snake of the eastern and central United States. The species is adult at about 2.5 feet (74 cm) in total length. Represented by five races, aberrant patterns are well documented in three of them: the southern (striped), the Osage (patternless), and the Trans-Pecos (connected dark blotches) copperheads.

Cottonmouths

The cottonmouth (three subspecies) is related to the copperhead. Juveniles are strongly patterned in a series of tan and brown bands, but adulthood brings with it a suffusion of melanin that all but obliterates the pattern of this large—to more than 4 feet (122 cm)—and heavy-bodied snake. Occurring in the southeastern and Mississippi drainage states, cottonmouths are associated with aquatic situations and are often referred to as water moccasins. The name cottonmouth is derived from the cottony white interior of the mouth, which is displayed when the snake feels threatened. Of the three races, albino eastern and western cottonmouths have been found and are now being bred in captivity. Because of the great degree of melanin normally present, albino cottonmouths are quite white in ground coloration and have yellowish markings.

Types of Cobra-Allies

Albinism also occurs in the cobra-allies of the family Elapidae. Because their fast-moving alertness makes them potentially more dangerous than the more lethargic viperine snakes, comparatively few cobra-allies are kept or bred by hobbyists.

One of the most commonly kept species is the monocled cobra, and it is in this 4- to 5-foot-long (122–152 cm) species that albinism is best documented. The alert demeanor, readiness to assume a typical cobra stance, milky white ground color, yellowish nape monocle, and pale red eyes render this a most impressive, and very dangerous, snake.

Among elapines albinism is also known to occur in the Texas coral snake, the banded krait, and the Australian yellow-faced whip-snake.

LIZARDS

It all started so innocently. Hobbyists found that leopard geckos bred fairly readily in captivity. After staring at hatched clutch after hatched clutch of baby geckos, a hobbyist said slowly, "Hey, some of these babies are more brightly colored than others . . ."

Leopard Geckos

For lizards, the one species that comes to mind when discussing color and pattern morphs is the leopard gecko, *Eublepharius macularis*. Originally from Pakistan and India, leopard geckos are denizens of dry desert areas or semiarid savannah areas. They are nocturnal, spending the day under rocks or in burrows of their own making. These are small-sized lizards, reaching an adult length of about 9 to 10 inches (23–25 cm).

Leopard geckos are essentially yellow lizards, with blotchy milk chocolate crossbands. As hatchlings, the bands are distinctly marked; they fade as the animal matures. The dorsal surface is liberally peppered with dark brown. Their skin is tuberculate, meaning it is dotted with raised nodules. The brown-spotted yellow head frequently has a semicircle of brown spots across the back of the head. The tail is heavy, arranged in whorls (distinct ridged circles), and easily broken. It regenerates, but never regains its original appearance. In a few examples, a vague orange suffusion appears at the base of the tail. When hunting insect prey, the tip of the tail is elevated and waved.

This is the pet lizard that every pet store owner, herpetophile, or beginner thinks of when asked, "What makes a nice pet lizard?" Leopard geckos are known for their hardiness, their ease of feeding, their attractive appearance, small size, and nocturnal habits. Males are very aggressive toward each other, so trios with a single male are the best way to house multiple animals. Leopard geckos don't bite except under extreme provocation, and their mouths are so small that no damage can be done. They breed so readily in captivity that the pet market is largely supplied with the captive-born progeny of captive-born progeny. Leopard geckos can live 15 to 22 years in captivity.

Breeding

Leopard geckos are one of the lizards with temperature-determined sex. If you want to

Albino leopard gecko.
(courtesy The Gourmet Rodent)

hatch a clutch comprised of mostly males, you incubate the leopard gecko eggs at 88 to 90°F (31–32.2°C); for females, you incubate the eggs at 83°F (28.3°C), or slightly lower. Clutches incubated at temperatures between these extremes, from 84 to 87°F (28.9–30.5°C), produce both males and females.

Morphs

With a steady supply of leopard geckos being cranked out each year, no wonder that some breeders scratched their respective heads and said, "Some of these babies are prettier than the others. Let's see what we can get by a little selective breeding." So the brighter leopards were pulled from multiple clutches, and bred to each other, and those young bred to each other.

✔ In the early 1990s a lizard with a lot of yellow coloring emerged, the high yellow morph. This lizard often had asymmetrical spotting. By 1996 a Florida breeder offered a high yellow leopard gecko with lavender bands.

✔ With commercial operations for leopard gecko production beginning in the 1990s, the lizard described as the jungle morph appeared.

This is a beautiful sandfire-phase inland bearded dragon, Pogona vitticeps.

Rather than being a banded lizard, the jungle morph had a marbled, asymmetrical pattern on its torso.

✔ Following the jungle morph, a striped morph appeared, with the bands now coalesced into an irregular stripe down the back. The striped morph was recessive to the jungle or wild pattern.

✔ Breeders then worked with the orange coloration, which occasionally appeared near the base of the tail on the normal, or wild-patterned, morphs. These appeared about 1994.

With these color morphs, still no albino appeared. But as with raising money, it's just a matter of trying enough times, of hatching enough leopard geckos. The first albino morphs, more accurately leucistic morphs, hatched from a group of imported leopard geckos in 1996. In 1997 and 1998 other members from that same imported group but belonging to different owners also produced some amelanistic young. Further breeding indicated that the amelanistic trait was governed by a single pair of alleles.

In 1998 the first patternless amelanistic morph was developed. This was a dark-eyed, unpatterned, pale-skinned leopard gecko.

In early 1996 a white gecko with dark blue-black eyes was hatched from normal-appearing parents. This baby was born white and patternless, unlike the leucistic patternless, which are born with a pattern that fades as the lizard matures. When mated with a patternless leucistic gecko, all normal young appeared, indicating that both genes were standard recessive.

The Gourmet Rodent is breeding albino leopard geckos, **Eublepharis macularius** *ssp. more colorful than many.*

But the patternless leucistic and the blizzard lizard genes can also act as codominant. In one breed of these two morphs, a gecko that showed both traits was hatched. It had a solid yellow body, the typical blizzard's gray head, indistinct gray mottling on the neck, and a white tail.

A red-eyed albino was captive-hatched in 1998. Three years later, striped, jungle, and lavender albinos have been produced. Are these lavender albinos some of the tyrosinase-positive albinos? We don't yet know. Further crossing has created the rainbow phase, with a brown and white mottled head, a yellow body with a few indistinct darker blotches and a few reduced brown spots, and the white-striped tail with brown spots along the sides. Breeding for more intensely orange and crossing with an albino has yielded the orange-banded gecko. It had a white body, yellow-orange legs, and yellow bands across the body. The top of the head is pale orange, mottled with white, and the eyes are red.

Darker Phase Leopards

The intense interest in the albino phases has sparked a like response toward the darker phase leopards. A black phase was shown at the Reptile Breeders' Expo in 1999.

Fat-tailed Geckos

The African fat-tailed gecko, *Hemitheconyx caudicinctus*, originally from Africa, also has color and pattern morphs. The fat-tail occurs naturally in two pattern morphs: the banded form, which has a dark brown body with broad yellow to buff bands, and a striped morph, a banded fat-tail with a white vertebral stripe. The first morphs to be developed were the leucistic and the albinistic.

Leucistic fat-tail: The leucistic fat-tail is a dark-eyed gecko with a pink-white ground color and yellow crossbands. Frequently the tail tip is a mottled white-pink. Of the two, the leucistic trait is the better established in breeding programs.

Khaki fat-tail: A color morph termed khaki displays a dark greenish ground color and dark brown bands. The khakis are not remarkable on their own, but can be a valuable addition to a breeding program. When a khaki fat-tail is bred to a leucistic morph, the white coloration of the young really stands out. The young are white lizards with white-to-ivory bands and a translucent opalescence to the skin. Darker or melanistic morphs of the fat-tail have also been developed, as have those with an intense orange ground color, with brown to orange-brown bands.

Knobtails

Leopard and fat-tailed geckos are by no means the only geckos being bred for new color and pattern morphs. There's a not so subtle shift into the more exotic species. New color morphs of exotic types, such as the knobtails (*Nephrurus laevis pibarensis*), double the "wow" factor. Knobtailed geckos are small lizards from Africa, found in mist microhabitats within arid areas. They are small, about 5 to 6 inches (13–15 cm) in total length, with a bulbous-tipped tail and the linchenate skin typical of many gecko genera. Don Hamper has bred patternless and albino knobtails.

Crested Geckos

Crested geckos, *Rhacodactylus ciliatus*, of New Caledonia, are one of the exotic geckos that has really taken hold in captive-breeding programs. These are fairly small lizards, reaching a total length of perhaps 8 to 9 inches (20–23 cm). Their tails are extremely friable. Seipp and Henkle reported seeing only regenerated tails on specimens seen in the wild.

Once thought to be extinct but rediscovered in 1994 and added to breeding programs, this is another lizard with enormous popular appeal. Perhaps the most distinctive characteristic of the crested gecko is the row of supraocular scales that make the lizard look like a cross between a flirtatious dance hall girl and Friar Tuck with his floppy rim of hair around the edge of his scalp. They have a wide range of natural colors, from gray, brown, green, and light yellow to an orange red. The fringe of scales over the eyes extend around the rear of the head, along the nape of the neck, and in a much reduced form, along each side of the back. The head and vertebral area enclosed by these lines is frequently paler than the body color. A few lizards may have a red gular area; this marking is not sexually dimorphic. Crested geckos feed mainly on fruits in the wild and convert readily to insects and fruits in captivity. Females lay paired eggs and may multiclutch. Calcium additives are especially important for egg-laying females.

Captive-born crested geckos are available in orange, yellow, red, peach, green, tiger, and fire morphs; frequently two colors are combined on a single lizard.

Bearded Dragons

The second most popular pet lizard is the bearded dragon. It has the pet attributes that hobbyists are looking for. It's large enough to handle, reaching an adult length of 14 inches

Herpetoculturists are selectively breeding to develop a very red strain of the New Caledonian crested gecko, **Rhacodactylus ciliatus.**

This albino neonate blue-tongued skink, Tiliqua scincoides ssp., was birthed by an imported female.

(36 cm). It's a cosmopolitan eater, living quite well on chopped mixed vegetables with a few mealworms now and then. The adults breed prolifically, laying large clutches of eggs twice a year. The normal pale tan coloration sometimes has a reddish tinge, sometimes a golden tinge, and that's all it takes to set hobbyists off into color morph breeding programs.

At first, heightened normal coloration was the goal: deeper golds, paler beiges, and more intense oranges and reds. By 1996 these were available commercially, as fire reds. A strongly contrasting phase, with darker crossbands against a paler background, was dubbed the tiger morph, and examples were available in 2000. That same year, other phases,

The recently developed "blizzard" phase of the leopard gecko has been a hit with hobbyists.

including leucistic, lime, and lavender, were being offered, as was a snow bearded.

Chinese Water Dragons

The Chinese water dragon, a normally green lizard with strong aquatic tendencies, often appears naturally with more intense blue tones to its coloration. Mike Spears of Sapphire Dragon Ranch has done some remarkable breeding work with this species, and has adults with turquoise blue bodies and kelly green legs.

Tegus

Tegus, *Tupinambis teguxin,* have also been bred to increase their blue coloration. The coloration intensifies as the tegu matures. The hatchlings are greenish gold with black bands; by the time they are 24 inches long (61 cm), at about six months, they are white with deep blue-black bands. Albino blue tegus, *Tupinambis teguxin* sp., are pale white with dark gray crossbands and markings and red eyes.

Skinks

Albino blue-tongued skinks, *Tiliqua scinciodes intermedia,* have been imported from New Guinea. These lizards are the usual heavy-bodied blue-tongued skink, but have pale pink bodies with yellow crossbands.

Dark as hatchlings, colors pale as blue tegus, **Tupinambis** *sp., attain their full size. Marian Bacon photographed these examples.*

Great Green Iguanas

The once-popular great green iguana is also available in a red-eyed albino morph. An adult albino was on display at the captive-breeding expo in 1995. Several albino hatchlings were in a shipment imported from Colombia in 1997. They were golden orange as babies, but the coloration faded to white as the animals matured. A captive-breeding program was delayed when one female died, egg bound, in 1999.

Hobbyists selectively breed to enhance the colors of inland bearded dragons, Pogona vitticeps. This very red morph was originated at Sandfire Dragon Ranch.

This leopard gecko has been selectively bred for its bright yellow coloration. (courtesy The Gourmet Rodent)

Nubbly, pink, and yellow describes this albino leopard gecko. (courtesy The Gourmet Rodent)

This albino fat-tailed gecko is just a few weeks old. (courtesy The Gourmet Rodent)

Although observers may not be able to easily identify a turtle or tortoise species, virtually everyone can identify them as a turtle. There are no other animals quite like these still-living relics from bygone eras.

Despite the fact that many turtles are predominantly aquatic—indeed, some come ashore only to lay eggs—they are reptiles, not amphibians as some may think. The shell is the trademark of turtles and tortoises. Hard and seemingly impervious to injury though it may seem, the shell is a living, growing, feeling structure. Some turtle species may periodically shed the outermost plate coverings, but the shell itself is never shed.

Types of Turtles

Albinism in turtles and tortoises has long been known, but has never been common. In the 1970s there was a canal in Largo, Florida, in which was found about a half dozen albino Florida snapping turtles, *Chelydra serpentina osceola*. These were starkly different from the normal brown ones found with them. Now surrounded by the city, this once remote drainage

The albino red-eared slider is especially visible at night.

system has produced no snapping turtles of any morph in many years.

A couple of albino desert tortoises, big brown tortoises of the Sonoran Desert, were hatched in the late 1960s, and although displayed by the Arizona-Sonora Desert Museum, they were not integrated into a breeding program. Both were a beautiful creamy white in color.

Single albino examples of several other turtle species have been found:

✔ Among these have been a beautiful eastern mud turtle, *Kinosternon s. subrubrum*, that was found in southeastern South Carolina. Normally colored adults are brown above and orange-brown below.

✔ An adult flattened musk turtle, *Sternotherus depressus*, now an endangered species, was found in an Alabama stream. This is typically a tannish brown turtle with darker streaks.

✔ A single albino of the normally nearly black common musk turtle, *Sternotherus odoratus*, has also been found. As far as is known, none of these have been selectively bred to perpetuate the trait.

✔ Rather recently an albino eastern box turtle, a turtle that ranges widely over much of the

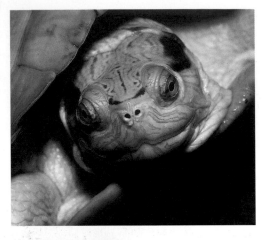

northeastern United States, has been found. The asking price is upward of $10,000! A few hypomelanistic eastern box turtles have been captive-produced. All are still juveniles, and since some pigment amounts increase with age, exactly what these turtles will look like as adults remains unknown.

TIP

Incubation Temperatures

The sex of many turtles is determined by the incubation temperature in the nest rather than genetically. Improper incubation temperatures can also result in altered color and pattern and in improper scute development. Since pastel red-ears are almost always females and almost always have deformed carapacial and plastral scutes, it is logical to assume that at least in the majority of the cases the color is incubation temperature-related.

Red-eared sliders, Trachemys scripta elegans, *have proven to be the most genetically plastic turtle species.*

Red-eared Sliders

Generally speaking, until Don Hamper and Clive Longden instituted captive-breeding programs for red-eared sliders in the 1980s, albino turtles were largely unknown. Although they may exceed 10 inches (25 cm) in carapace length when adult, red-ears have long been favorite pet turtles and are farmed by the hundreds of thousands for the pet trade. They are indigenous to the Mississippi drainage area but released pets have become established from Japan to southern Canada. At this time red-ears remain the only designer turtles routinely available. Albinos (now common), leucistics (still very rare), and some curiously colored and patterned "pastels" have been produced. The first two of these, the albinos and leucistics, are genetically derived. It is likely that the latter, the various pastel phases, result largely, if not entirely, from manipulated incubation temperatures. However, exotic turtle breeder Rick Van Dyke feels that at least some of the pastel colors, most notably the tannish morph now referred to as a ghost, may truly be genetic mutations.

Florida Red-bellied Turtles

Pastel colorations are also known in Florida red-bellied turtles, *Pseudemys nelsoni.* These turtles have a shell length of about 12 inches (30 cm) when adult. As with the red-ears, when incubated at high temperatures, shell and occasionally tail deformities are not uncommon.

Clive Longden has been working for more than a decade to stabilize albinism in the common snapping turtle, Chelydra serpentina serpentina.

Common Snapping Turtles

Red-eared sliders may not be the sole albino turtle species available for much longer. For several years Clive Longden has been accruing albino turtles of many species, but has concentrated primarily on acquiring and breeding albino common snapping turtles. His project was set back some when after sizing and breeding two albino snappers, the hatchlings produced were all of normal brown coloration. From this event it became evident that even though both of the parents were albinos, the albinism was caused by two different genetic factors. However, all of the babies should have been heterozygous for both types of albinism. These have been sized and bred, and Longden is hoping for his first clutches of albino snappers

this year (2001). The single drawback to snapping turtles is size; an adult can exceed 55 pounds (25 kg) in weight and have a shell over a foot (30 cm) in length.

Map Turtles and Painted Turtles

Both albinism and hypomelanism have occurred in map turtles from the Mississippi drainage area and albinism is well documented in painted turtles in both the northeastern and northwestern United States. The map turtles attain a moderate size (females to 10 inches [25 cm], males to 6 inches [15 cm]) and the painted turtles are usually in the 5- to 7-inch (13–18 cm) size range when adult. Clive Longden now has plans for selective breeding programs for both Mississippi map turtles, *Graptemys pseudogeographica kohni,* and false map turtles, *G. p. pseudogeographica,* as well as western painted turtles, *Chrysemys picta bellii,* and midland painted turtles, *C. p. marginata.*

Florida Soft-shelled Turtles

Albinos of the Florida soft-shelled turtle, *Apalone (Trionyx) ferox*, are occasionally found. When babies these are endearing creatures that are astoundingly agile in the water, their chosen medium. The hatchlings are prettily colored in strawberry and cream tones. As they grow the colors fade, and by the time they are 6 or 8 inches long (15–20 cm), they are basically white. Should you choose to acquire one of these, be ready to give it a very large aquarium. Adults may exceed 75 pounds (34 kg) in weight—one was 96 pounds (43.5 kg)!—and 20 inches (51 cm) in length.

Asian Black-rayed Soft-shelled Turtles

Hypomelanistic examples of the tannish brown Asian black-rayed soft-shelled turtle, *Amyda (Trionyx) cartilaginea*, are rather frequently available in the American pet market. These are white turtles that often bear a variable amount of black on the carapace. They have dark eyes. This species attains a length of about a foot (30 cm), and is often very defensive, biting savagely when handled.

Albinism is now well documented in the Florida soft-shelled turtle, **Apalone ferox.**

Asian Giant Wood Turtles

The Asian giant wood turtle, *Heosemys grandis*, is one of the larger Asian species to enter the American pet trade. Normally clad in hues of dark brown, the occasional albino is a creamy yellow and white. These huge turtles may exceed 20 pounds (9.1 kg) in weight and 16 inches (41 cm) in length. They feed equally well on land or in water, but do enjoy soaking and swimming occasionally. Should you acquire a giant wood turtle, be aware that they are excellent climbers and escape artists, easily scaling fences 4 or 5 feet (122–152 cm) in height.

Types of Tortoises

Tortoises are land-dwelling turtles that seldom voluntarily swim. Most species have highly domed carapaces and many are the favorites of herpetoculturists.

Examples of the Asian black-rayed soft-shelled turtle, Amyda cartilageneus, *colored in this manner are marketed as "calicoes."*

Richard Fife of Riparian Farms was ecstatic when hypomelanistic (albino?) hatchlings appeared in his breeding programs with African spurred tortoises, Geochelone sulcata.

Besides the desert tortoise mentioned earlier, two additional species that may have aberrant colors are present in the pet trade.

These are the African spurred tortoise, *Geochelone sulcata*, and the South American red-footed tortoise, *Geochelone carbonaria*.

Spurred tortoise: The spurred tortoise is the largest of the mainland tortoises. Males, the larger sex, may attain a weight of more than 100 pounds (45 kg) and a length of more than 2 feet (61 cm). The normal coloration of the spurred tortoise is brown with tan to light brown centers of the carapacial scutes. Recently (2000) a hypomelanistic morph, dubbed the ivory tortoise by its breeder Richard Fife, has become available. Currently the asking price for hatchling ivory tortoises is $10,000 each.

Red-footed tortoise: The red-footed tortoise is one of the most commonly seen tortoise species in captivity. It is usually quite dark with light centers in each carapacial scute and a variable amount of red or orange on the head and forelimbs.

Occasionally specimens with light radiating marks in each carapacial scute, or even more rarely, having a solid ivory or tan carapace, are encountered. So far none of these interesting phases have been incorporated into successful breeding programs, but it is probably only a matter of time before this is done.

TWO CROCODILIANS

Except for turtles, the American alligator, Alligator mississippiensis, *may be the most readily recognized reptile in the United States.*

In bygone decades the alligator was common to abundant in waterways of the southeastern states, and attained a length of more than 15 feet (4.6 m); the record size was 19 feet 2 inches (5.8 m)! Then, due to hunting and other pressures in the 1950s and 1960s, the population of these creatures plummeted to such lows that it was almost impossible to find one. When the Endangered Species Act was passed, American alligators became a prime species for inclusion thereon. Thus protected, the big reptiles began a population rebound, until today (2001) they are again a common sight throughout much of the Southeast. As a matter of fact, on a warm sunny day when water levels are moderately low, a visitor to Paynes Prairie State Preserve in north central Florida can often see from several dozen to several hundred alligators sunning along the canals.

Typically, American alligators are black banded with bright yellow at hatching, but the yellow fades with growth and adults are olive black to almost jet black.

Types of Aberrant Colors in Crocodilians

Then, in 1987, in a marshland in Louisiana, a number of white hatchling alligators were found by a fisherman. A few were collected and given to the Audubon Zoo in New Orleans; others are maintained by other organizations. All are now young adults.

These white alligators are leucistic—pure ivory white with blue eyes. Some have small dark spots on the head. Leucism has proven to be a heritable mutation in some reptile species, and it is hoped that it will prove to be so in American alligators. Besides leucism, albino American alligators have been found. These are a yellowish white with pinkish red eyes.

Aberrant colors are known in a few other crocodilians as well. One of the most striking examples is a pure white spectacled caiman, *Caiman crocodilus* ssp., an alligator relative. Spectacled caiman range from Mexico throughout much of northern South America. They are small—6 to 8 feet (1.8–2.4 m) but what they lack in size, they more than make up in feistiness.

Because of their potential size, many municipalities and some states now prohibit the keeping of crocodilians by private hobbyists. However, crocodilians of many species, including the leucistic ones from Louisiana, are maintained at many zoological parks. A large alligator is impressive even when normally colored; the white ones are nothing short of spectacular!

Albino spectacle caiman. (from the Clive Longden Collection)

AMPHIBIANS

Because their responses to breeding are so very closely tied to environmental cues such as rain, humidity, and photoperiod, amphibians are not as routinely captive-bred as reptiles. In fact, comparatively few appear with any regularity.

In the pet trade, the color and pattern anomalies of amphibians are poorly documented. Only three anomalies are reported with any degree of regularity: albinism in varying degrees (including hypomelanism), leucism, and axanthism.

Albinism in Amphibians

Of the three, it is albinism that is best studied, and is most often seen in wild amphibians. Albinism is so prominently established in African clawed frogs that when seen in that species it is seldom commented on. It is now almost the norm in axolotls (leucistic examples of this salamander are also common), Chaco horned frogs, and American bullfrogs.

Albino specimens of both northern and southern leopard frogs, and an occasional tiger

Blue coloration in amphibians may be the result of axanthism, but can also occur when diets lack sufficient beta carotene. Pictured is a painted-bellied monkey frog, Phyllomedusa sauvagei.

salamander are also occasionally found and collected from the wild, but have so far been seldom captive-bred.

Two of the newest and the most exciting of the albino amphibians to enter the pet trade are the American green treefrog and the red-eyed treefrog. Only a few of these hobbyist favorites are yet available and as of mid-2001 the prices asked for either remain very high. However, as abinos of both species become more routinely available, the prices should drop drastically.

Blue, rather than green, examples of several other species of amphibians—Mexican leaf-frogs, painted-bellied monkey frogs, White's (dumpy) treefrogs, and green frogs among them—are occasionally found. Experiments have shown that in some cases green to blue color changes can be induced by withholding dietary beta carotene, but in other instances the coloration is genetically caused by axanthism, a deficiency of yellow that, when mixed with the blue, creates normally seen green.

Bispecific hybrids of another horned frog, dubbed the fantasy frog, are also readily available in the pet trade. This is a hybrid between the ornate and the Suriname horned frog.

Types of Frogs

Horned Frogs

Together with close relatives, the horned frogs form a subfamily (the Ceratophryinae) of a huge assemblage of tropical frogs known as the leptodactylids. There have probably never been any other frog species that have caught the fancy of hobbyists like these squat, terrestrial, big-headed, and voracious anurans. Horned frogs are sit-and-wait predators, usually concealing themselves and eating any large insects, other frogs, or even small mammals that happen by. These frogs burrow extensively, and those species that dwell where there is an extended dry season are capable of undergoing a period of quiescence wrapped in a moisture-retaining cocoon of dried skin and skin secretions. The frogs again become active when rains wet the ground and breed when ephemeral puddles are filled.

There are more than a half dozen species of horned frogs, but only two of the larger species—the ornate horned frog and the Chaco horned frog (both from southern South America)—are consistently available in the pet trade. The females of both are large and impressive, attaining a length of 4 or 5 inches (10–13 cm) and an even greater breadth. The males are much smaller. Once sexual maturity is attained, the sexes are easily determined, the males

Albino Chaco horned frogs, Ceratophrys cranwelli, *have been established in captivity since the 1980s.*

being notably less robust and having a dark throat.

Of the two, the ornate horned frog, *Ceratophrys ornata*, seems the more normally variable in coloration but it is the Chaco horned frog, *Ceratophrys cranwelli*, in which albinism has occurred. In the wild the Chaco horned frog is normally a well-camouflaged earthen brown in coloration. Captive-breeding projects have now lightened the browns, added greens, and produced a line of very pretty yellow to white albinos.

The Fantasy Frog

The fantasy frog is a bispecific hybrid between *C. ornata and C. cornuta*. This pretty frog is rather smooth-skinned and has supraorbital horns that are longer than those of the ornate, but shorter than the long appendages typically borne by the Suriname horned frog. It is also intermediate in size between the two. This is usually a very fast-growing, robust, and hardy frog that is now readily available to hobbyists at inexpensive prices.

Treefrogs

Of the hobbyists' four favorite treefrog species, three occasionally display blue rather than green coloration and albinos of the third have only recently appeared in the American pet trade.

The three species prone to blue coloration are the Mexican leaffrog, *Pachymedusa dacnicolor*, of Mexico, the painted-bellied monkey frog, *Phyllomedusa sauvagii*, of temperate southern South America, and White's (dumpy) treefrog, *Litoria caerulea*, of Australia and Indonesia. Albinos and leucistic specimens of the red-eyed treefrog, *Agalychnis callidryas*,

of southern Mexico and Central America, are now known. All are in the family Hylidae, the true treefrogs.

Despite the fact that all of these frogs are capable of leaping long distances, they seldom

TIP

Diet and Care
✔ Despite the fact that many of the larger frogs—all of the horned frogs, White's treefrogs, Mexican leaffrogs, and American bullfrogs, among them—will readily eat pinky and slightly larger mice, these high-fat morsels should be offered only as an occasional "treat." A diet high in fat has recently been implicated in corneal lipid deposits, irreversible fatty corneal deposits that cause blindness.
✔ A varied diet of crickets, roaches, minnows, and earthworms is suggested.
✔ Most frogs are cannibalistic. Either keep them separated or keep only those of similar sizes together.
✔ Because frogs and salamanders have permeable skins, chemicals, including those from waste products, can be absorbed and cause disease and death. The quarters in which your amphibians are maintained must be immaculately clean.
✔ Use no phenol-based cleansers when cleaning and sterilizing caging. Chlorine-based cleansers are somewhat safer, but must be *thoroughly* rinsed from the cage before the amphibians are reintroduced.

Matt Lerer photographed these two (albino and normal) red-eyed treefrogs, **Agalychnis callidryas.**

to noncaptive conditions has resulted in some states passing regulations forbidding the possession of these frogs. Besides albinos, this interesting, but very predaceous, aquatic frog occurs in its normal muddy-colored morph, a leucistic coloration, piebald, and at least one phase that has an interestingly busy dark dorsal pattern against a tan body color.

Clawed frogs are more often seen housed in aquarium sections than with the reptiles and amphibians in pet shops. Most often available as inch-long (25 mm) babies, if fed properly clawed frogs can attain their adult 4-inch (10 cm) length quite quickly. They may live as long as 20 years in captivity. Although compatible with most fish when small, as they grow the frogs will begin eating most finned tankmates. They also eat prepared pelleted fishfoods.

do, more often treading their arboreal highways in a methodical hand-over-hand, foot-over-foot mode of movement.

When in good condition, three of these species—the Mexican leaffrog, so called because it places its egg masses above the water on leaves and grasses, the painted-bellied monkey frog, named for the dexterity its opposing thumb provides, and the White's treefrog—are rather corpulent in appearance. It is necessary to limit their food intake in captivity to assure that they do not become obese.

The red-eyed treefrog is a slender species that is somewhat more active then the other discussed species and is less apt to become overweight. A very few leucistic specimens have been noted, but not until recently have albino examples occurred. These latter are creamy white with the typical red eyes.

African Clawed (Underwater) Frogs

Albino clawed frogs have been available to hobbyists for so many years that they are now all but overlooked. Their extreme adaptability

Typical Frogs

The so-called "typical frogs" are members of the large and widely distributed family Ranidae. They are streamlined in appearance, accomplished long-distance leapers, and often nervous captives. Most are associated with permanent water sources or damp meadows. The four species occasionally seen in the American pet trade are native to North America. Although none of these have been routinely kept by hobbyists, the current availability of albino examples of the long-lived American bullfrog, *Rana catesbeiana*, at relatively inexpensive prices is changing this.

Besides the bullfrog, the northern leopard frog, *Rana pipiens*, and the southern leopard frog, *Rana sphenocephala*, also occur in an albino morph. The fourth, the green frog, *Rana clamitans melanota*, occurs in an axanthic (yellow coloration suppressed) blue phase.

Types of Salamanders

Salamanders are for the most part small, retiring denizens of cool, moist woodlands. Some are fully terrestrial, not even needing ponds in which to breed. Others are burrowing species that require standing water in which to deposit eggs and in which their gilled larvae grow, develop, and metamorphose. A few are fully aquatic. Except for the axolotl, an aquatic Mexican mole (ambystomatid) salamander, few salamanders are bred by American hobbyists. Additionally, they are so secretive, that comparatively few are collected from the wild for the hobby. It is no wonder, then, that although albinism and melanism are occasionally reported in salamanders, it is seldom seen except in the axolotl.

Axolotls: The axolotl, *Ambystoma mexicanum*, is a paedomorphic (permanently larval) salamander. Its closest relative among the salamanders of the United States is the tiger salamander, *Ambystoma tigrinum* ssp. Despite the fact that it never develops the glandular skin or eyelids of an adult mole salamander, and retains three pairs of bushy gills throughout its life, the axolotl does attain sexual maturity.

Axolotls are usually readily available in a pretty golden white albino (with pink eyes)

*The genetics of the axolotls, **Ambystoma mexicana**, are very well researched. An albino example is pictured.*

morph and a black-eyed white leucistic morph as well as piebald and normal (olive-mud) colors.

Tiger salamanders: Because they are large and often colorful, and easily kept, but not so easily bred, tiger salamanders are favorites of many hobbyists. Albinos of several of the six subspecies have been found. On those races having prominent "tigerlike" markings, the ground color of the albinos is often purplish gray and the markings are cream to yellow.

Albinos and Piebalds

Albinos of several of the lungless salamanders (plethodontids) have also been found but have never been bred in captivity. Among others, albino examples of red-backed and dusky salamanders have been reported.

Other than on axolotls, the only incidence of piebaldism that we have seen is on a large example of the two-toed amphiuma (*Amphiuma means*) now in the collection of Riverbanks Zoo in Columbia, South Carolina. This interesting eel-like salamander was thought to be a "white snake" when found by a homeowner in a suburban Columbia, South Carolina backyard.

GLOSSARY

See also Helpful Terms to Know, page 15.

Aestivation A period of warm weather inactivity; often triggered by excessive heat or drought.

Ambient temperature The temperature of the surrounding environment.

Amelanistic Lacking black pigment.

Amplexus The breeding grasp.

Anerythristic Lacking red pigment.

Anterior Toward the front.

Anus The external opening of the cloaca; the vent.

Boid A python or boa.

Carapace The upper shell of a turtle or tortoise.

Caudal Pertaining to the tail.

cb/cb Captive-bred, captive-born.

cb/ch Captive-bred, captive-hatched.

Cloaca The common chamber into which digestive, urinary, and reproductive systems empty and that itself opens exteriorly through the vent or anus.

Colubrine/Colubridae The largest of the snake groupings, containing such snakes as garters, rats, kings, and gophers.

Constricting Wrapping tightly in coils and squeezing.

Deposition As used here, the laying of the eggs.

Deposition site The spot chosen by the female to lay her eggs.

Dichromatic Two color phases of the same species, often sex-linked.

Dimorphic A difference in form, build, or coloration involving the same species; often sex-linked.

Diurnal Active in the daytime.

Dopa A chemical integral to the synthesis of melanin (3,4 dihydroxy-L-phenylalanine).

Dorsal Pertaining to the back; upper surface.

Dorsolateral Pertaining to the upper sides.

Dorsum The upper surface.

Ecological niche The precise habitat utilized by a species.

Ectothermic "Cold-blooded"; also poikilothermic.

Endothermic "Warm-blooded."

Erythristic A prevalence of red pigment.

Form An identifiable species or subspecies.

Fossorial Adapted for burrowing; a burrowing species.

Genus A taxonomic classification of a group of species having similar characteristics. The genus falls between the next higher designation of "family" and the next lower designation of "species." Genera is the singular of genus. The generic name is always capitalized when written.

Glottis The opening of the windpipe.

Gravid The reptilian equivalent of mammalian pregnancy.

Gular Pertaining to the throat.

Heliothermic Pertaining to a species that basks in the sun to thermoregulate.

Hemipenes The dual copulatory organs of male lizards and snakes.

Hemipenis The singular form of hemipenes.

Herpetoculture The captive-breeding of reptiles and amphibians.

Herpetoculturist One who indulges in herpetoculture.

Herpetologist One who indulges in herpetology.

Herpetology The study, often scientifically oriented, of reptiles and amphibians.

Hibernacula Winter dens.

Hibernation Winter dormancy; also called brumation.

Hybrid Offspring resulting from the breeding of two species or two noncontiguous subspecies.

Hydrate To restore body moisture by drinking or absorption.

Hydration chamber An enclosed high humidity chamber used to help desiccated frogs rehydrate.

Intergrade Offspring resulting from the breeding of two contiguous subspecies.

Juvenile A young or immature specimen.

Keel A ridge (along the center of a scale).

Labial Pertaining to the lips.

Lampropeltine A snake of the subfamily Lampropeltinae; pine, bull, gopher, king, milk, rat, and related snakes.

Lateral Pertaining to the side.

Melanism A profusion of black pigment.

Middorsal Pertaining to the middle of the back.

Midventral Pertaining to the center of the belly or abdomen.

Natricine A snake of the subfamily Natricinae; garter, ribbon, water, and related species.

Nocturnal Active at night.

Nuptial excrescence The roughened thumb, wrist, and forearm grasping pads of reproductively active male anurans.

Ontogenetic Age-related (color) changes.

Oviparous Reproducing by means of eggs that hatch after laying.

Photoperiod The daily/seasonally variable length of the hours of daylight.

Plastron The bottom shell of a turtle or tortoise.

Posterior Toward the rear.

Postocular Posterior to the eye.

Preocular Anterior to the eye.

Race A subspecies.

Ranid A true frog.

Rostral The (often modified) scale on the tip of the snout.

Scute A large scale or scalelike plate.

Species A group of similar creatures that produce viable young when breeding; the taxonomic designation that falls beneath genus and above subspecies.

Subspecies The subdivision of a species; a race that may differ slightly in color, size, scalation, or other criteria.

Sympatric Occurring together.

Taxonomy The science of classification of plants and animals.

Terrestrial Land-dwelling.

Thermoregulate To regulate (body) temperature by choosing a warmer or cooler environment.

Thigmothermic Pertaining to a species (often nocturnal) that thermoregulates by being in contact with a preheated surface such as a boulder or tarred road surface.

Tympanum The external eardrum.

Vent The external opening of the cloaca; the anus.

Venter The underside of a creature; the belly.

Ventral Pertaining to the undersurface or belly.

Ventrolateral Pertaining to the sides of the venter (belly).

INFORMATION

Books

Bechtel, Bernard H. *Reptile and Amphibian Variants: Colors, Patterns and Scales.* Malabar, Florida: Kreiger, 1995.

Broghammer, Stefan. *Albinos: Color and Pattern Mutations of Snakes and Other Reptiles.* Frankfurt, Germany: M&S Verlag, 2000.

De Vosjoli, Philippe; Klingenberger, Roger, DVM; Barker, David; Barker, Tracy. *The Ball Python Manual.* Santee, California: The Herpetoculturists Library, 1995.

De Vosjoli, Philippe; Klingenberger, Roger, DVM; Ronne, Jeff. *The Boa Constrictor Manual.* Santee, California: The Herpetoculturists Library, 1998.

De Vosjoli, Philippe; Viets, Brian; Tremper, Ron; Klingenberger, Roger, DVM. *The Leopard Gecko Manual.* Santee, California: The Herpetoculturists Library, 1998.

Love, Kathy and Love, Bill. *The Corn Snake Manual.* Santee, California: The Herpetoculturists Library, 2000.

Magazines

Reptile and Amphibian Magazine
RD 3, Box 3709-A
Pottsville, PA 17901

Reptiles Magazine
P.O. Box 6050
Mission Viejo, CA 92690-6050

The Vivarium
P.O. Box 300067
Escondido, CA 92030-0067
(Available by membership in American Federation of Herpetoculturists)

Reptilian
22 Firs Close
Hazlemere, High Wycombe
Bucks HP15 7TF, England

Reptile Hobbyist
P.O. Box 427
Neptune, NJ 07753

The following professional journals are available only to members of the societies or, occasionally, through used book sellers.

Herpetological Review and the *Journal of Herpetology*
The Society for the Study of Reptiles and Amphibians
Department of Zoology
Miami University
Oxford, OH 45056

Copeia
The American Society of Ichthyologists and Herpetologists
Department of Zoology
Southern Illinois University
Carbondale, IL 62901-6501

Herpetologica
c/o Maureen A. Donnelly
College of Arts and Sciences
Florida International University
North Miami, FL 33181

Herp Websites

American Society of Ichthyologists and
   Herpetologists
www.utexas.edu/depts/asih/

Society for the Study of Reptiles and Amphibians
http://falcon.cc.ukans.edu/~gpisani/SSAR.html

Herp pictures
http://gto.ncsa.uinc.edu/pingleto/lobby.html

Michigan Museum of Zoology
http://www.ummz.lsa.imich.edu.herps/

International Public Library Ready Reference
http://www.ipl.org/ref/RR/static/ent6580.html

This albino prairie rattlesnake,
Crotalus viridis viridis, *from the*
Ryan Blakely collection, was
photographed by Mike Price.

INDEX

Important Note

While handling amphibians and reptiles, you may occasionally receive bites or scratches. If your skin is broken, contact your physician immediately.

Amphibians and reptiles may transmit certain infections to humans. Always wash your hands carefully after handling your specimens. And always supervise children who wish to observe or handle your amphibians or reptiles.

About the Authors

Patricia Bartlett is the author of 25 books on Florida history and natural history. She writes regularly for national magazines on pet shop management as well as reptile and amphibian husbandry.

R. D. Bartlett, a herpetologist, has authored numerous articles and books on reptile and amphibian field identification and husbandry. He travels and lectures extensively, and guides tours to the Amazon. In 1978, he began the Reptile Breeding and Research Institute, a private facility. Since RBRI's inception, more than 150 species have been bred, some for the first time in the United States under captive conditions.

Acknowledgments

Our sincerest thanks to Bern and Bette Bechtel, longtime researchers into color aberrancies of reptiles and amphibians, and to Tom Boyden who introduced me (RDB) to my first albino Sonoran gopher snakes. Thanks also to Bill and Marcia Brant and Joe Hiduke of The Gourmet Rodent, one of the nation's largest breeders of designer snakes; to Dennis Cathcart who was with Patti and me when we collected our first and only albino corn snake; and to Scott Cushnir, connoisseur snake breeder. We must also extend thanks to Rob MacInnes, Chuck Hurt, and Mike Stuhlman of Glades Herp, Inc.; to Bill and Kathy Love, who together own CornUtopia; to Chris McQuade and Sheila Rodgers of Gulf Coast Reptiles; to Paul Hollander, and to Rich and Connie Zuchowski, proprictors of Serpenco. Our appreciation must also be extended to Marian Bacon, Doug Beckwith, Chris Bednarski, Cheryl Bott, Mark Cantos, Terry Dunham, Mike Ellard, Matt Lerer, Justin Garza, Don Hamper, Clive Longden, Bob Maillioux, Regis Opferman, Mike Price, and Kenny Wray who allowed us to photograph, provided information about, or provided photographs of the many wonderfully colored aberrant reptiles and amphibians with which they work.

Special thanks also to Frank Indiviglio for a thoughtful evaluation of the initial manuscript, and to our editor, Dave Rodman, for treading masterfully through our dangling participles and split infinitives.

Cover Photos

R. D. Bartlett

Photo Credits

Marion Bacon: page 74; R. D. Bartlett: all photos except those credited to other photographers; Matt Lerer: pages 24, 64, and 88; Clive Longdon: page 82; Bob Mailloux: page 12; Carl May: page 19 (bottom); and Mike Price: pages 29, 59, 66, and 93.

All inquiries should be addressed to:
Barron's Educational Series, Inc.
250 Wireless Boulevard
Hauppauge, NY 11/88
http://www.barronseduc.com

International Standard Book No. 0-7641-1706-8

Library of Congress Catalog Card No. 2001043358

Library of Congress Cataloging-in-Publication Data
Bartlett, Richard D., 1938–
    Designer reptiles and amphibians / Richard and Patricia Bartlett.
        p. cm.
    Includes bibliographical references (p.).
    ISBN 0-7641-1706-8 (alk. paper)
        1. Reptiles as pets. 2. Amphibians as pets.
    I. Bartlett, Patricia Pope, 1949– II. Title.
SF459.R4 D37 2002
639.3'9—dc21   2001043358

Printed in Hong Kong
9 8 7 6 5 4 3 2 1